MW01287257

LOOK
UP

GLOBAL STORIES
OF RESILIENCE

LOOK UP
GLOBAL STORIES OF RESILIENCE

HEIDI SIEFKAS

Copyright © 2025 by Heidi Siefkas

All Rights Reserved. No part of this publication may be reproduced, distributed, or transmitted in any form or by any means, including photocopying, recording, or other electronic or mechanical methods, without the prior written permission of the author, except in the case of brief quotations embodied in reviews and certain other noncommercial uses permitted by copyright law. Direct requests for permission to *heidi@hidenseekmedia.com.*

Editing: Peggy Henrikson, Heart and Soul Editing
Cover and Interior Design: Yvonne Parks, PearCreative.ca

Printed in the United States of America

LCCN: 2024925612

ISBN: 978-0-9971963-7-5 (paperback)
ISBN: 978-0-9971963-8-2 (ebook)

Also by Heidi Siefkas

When All Balls Drop: The Upside of Losing Everything (2014)
With New Eyes: The Power of Perspective (2015)
Cubicle to Cuba: Desk Job to Dream Job (2016)

DEDICATION

I dedicate this book to all my contributors who shared a personal story. By doing so, it keeps those stories alive so that we all can learn, facing adversity and triumphing against odds, whatever comes our way.

A special thanks to my clan of supporters, both family and friends, who come from all walks of life. Whether you are near, far, or in your version of Paradise, you were crucial in my triumph.

Here's to looking up!

CONTENTS

PROLOGUE
HEIDI SIEFKAS

My life has been full of much love and many adventures, as well as several unforeseen and traumatic hardships. My journey is a testament to the unyielding power of resilience and the insight of perspective, themes that run through my memoir *When All Balls Drop* and continue to shape my life today. My story is not just about survival but transformation—about how I chose to look up in the face of overwhelming odds, not once but multiple times. *Look Up—Global Stories of Resilience* seeks to bring this mindset to a worldwide audience, showcasing the paths of individuals from all walks of life who have overcome adversity, proving that through hardship, we gain wisdom.

LIFE INTERRUPTED BY A TREE

In 2009, while visiting the Hudson River Valley, New York, I stepped outside a rental apartment to take out the trash. Little did I know that this task would change my life forever. A tree limb crashed down on me, leaving me with a broken neck and several severe injuries. A good Samaritan found me unconscious, and an ambulance rushed me to the local trauma hospital.

Fortunately, I survived an accident that could have killed me, but in the process, my entire life as I knew it was about to change. My once vibrant, active lifestyle had come to a sudden halt—health, marriage, and career all in jeopardy.

Despite the trauma, my first response was not to succumb to despair. Instead, I chose to focus on recovery, leaning into the power of looking up, both literally and figuratively. "Your accident wasn't a life change," a doctor told me. "The life change will be the path you choose because of your gained perspective." This advice would come to define my journey forward.

As I began to heal from my physical wounds, I also started to heal emotionally and mentally. I coined the term or mantra *Look Up* to capture my new approach to life—a mindset focused on being present in the moment and finding the upside in even the most difficult circumstances. The mantra became a way for me to not only cope with my recovery but also to inspire others.

My story, as recounted in *When All Balls Drop* as well as my TEDx talk, details how I recovered physically and regained my independence. It tells of how I navigated a life that no longer looked like the one I had planned. Through it all, I remained committed to *Look Up*, which encouraged me to embrace each moment for what it was—whether joyful or painful—and to seek out the lessons hidden within the hardship.

ANOTHER TRAGEDY: LOSS STRIKES AGAIN

My resilience would be tested again, in one of the most heartbreaking ways possible. In 2022, my partner Brian tragically lost his life in a plane crash off the coast of Maui. For twelve years, he had been my anchor and my "partner in crime," and in an instant, he was gone and the life we had planned together vanished.

The grief was overwhelming, and for many months, it seemed as if *Look Up* might not be enough to pull me through this time. Nevertheless, I leaned on the lessons from my previous journey of healing. I knew that even in this immense loss, there had to be something I could hold onto—something that would guide me forward.

LOOK UP—GLOBAL STORIES OF RESILIENCE, THE BOOK

My personal story is the spark that inspired this book, but it's just one of many. This collection of stories showcases individuals from the far reaches of the globe who have faced immense challenges and found the strength to persevere. These stories highlight the power of perspective and the incredible resilience of the human spirit. From war survivors to those battling illness, from personal tragedies to professional setbacks, each story in the book serves as a reminder that no matter what happens, we can choose how we respond and evolve to a stronger self.

The *Look Up* mantra has two main components: The first is to be present in the moment, to truly see both the beauty and the hazards around us; the second is to find the upside in every obstacle, knowing that wounds will eventually turn into wisdom. Each story in *Look Up—Global Stories of Resilience* reinforces these ideas, showing that no matter the hardship, there's always a way to find your inner champion (aka badass) and expand into a new life.

Both my personal life and this book of stories demonstrate that while we can't always control what happens to us, we *can* control how we frame a situation by tapping into the power of perspective. These stories serve as a mighty reminder that even in the darkest moments, we have the ability to choose hope, to be resilient, and to look up.

Highly influential for me in coming to terms with all of life's hurdles and gifts was Joseph Campbell's quote, "We must be willing to let go of the life we planned so as to have the life that is waiting for us." This is a universal truth. When life knocks us down, it's our choice to stay down or to rise, stronger and wiser from the experience.

PART 1:

TRANSFORMING LOSS AND PAIN INTO PURPOSE

LAHAINA RISING
PAMELA READER

Pamela and her husband Keenan had lived on Maui, the Valley Isle, for twenty-four years, raising their daughters, Kaia and Ellie, in a tight-knit Lahaina neighborhood. Their home was a labor of love, a fixer-upper that evolved little by little alongside their family. Their life was filled with school routines, shared sunsets, and neighborhood camaraderie. "Our neighborhood was more than a place," she said; "it was a community where everyone looked out for one another."

But on August 8, 2023, everything changed.

THE DAY OF THE FIRE

The day started with unusual weather. A hurricane 800 miles south of the island stirred strong winds. That morning, the family lost power, a minor inconvenience, which was quite common on the island, and they initially shrugged it off. The girls' school closed for the day; thus, Keenan, who's the school's college counselor, stayed home. He used the unexpected day off to work on a long-planned deck project. Pamela described the day as oddly reminiscent of a snow day in New York City, where she grew up: "It was cozy. The girls and I, along with my sister-in-law, niece, and nephew, played games and just spent time together."

But as the winds intensified, conditions turned unsettling, with dry terrain, unbridled winds, and talk of an earlier fire that had been extinguished. By afternoon, shingles were flying off nearby roofs. Windows shattered under the force of debris. Smoke began to rise ominously on the horizon, a reminder of the morning fire, perhaps its embers being fueled by the abnormally powerful winds.

Now without cell service or power and with the flying debris, Pamela decided it might be prudent to pack a few essentials, recalling a previous fire in 2018 when they'd evacuated briefly. The family loaded the car with hastily chosen items: clothes, food, and a fireproof envelope containing important documents. "There was no part of me that thought we were leaving forever," Pamela said later.

As the smoke thickened and flames crept closer, their neighborhood faced the agonizing question: Stay or go? Many neighbors believed the roads were impassable and chose to stay.

Suddenly, a friend of the family's, Anthony, a young Maui County lifeguard they knew from New York, rolled up on a little kid's bike. Black soot covering his face, he yelled, "It's time to go!" Like Anthony, Keenan serves as an ocean lifeguard in New York during summers. He's always extra calm during trying situations—sometimes to the point of mildly annoying Pamela and the girls. However, when Anthony instructed them to leave and Keenan looked at him and back at his family, they all knew this was serious. The girls immediately ran outside and saw frightening flames just two blocks away.

CARAVAN TO EVACUATE

Pamela and the girls quickly jumped into one vehicle with the cat, and Keenan followed in another vehicle. The plan was to get far enough away to reevaluate the situation without losing sight of one another. The evacuation was harrowing—and something they will never forget. They passed families walking with suitcases, a surreal image against the backdrop of chaos. Pamela described the moment: "It felt like a scene from a movie. People were fleeing on foot, dragging what little they could carry. We were driving through an apocalypse."

Worried about their home, they took shelter on the outskirts of town around 6 p.m., within sight of their community and close to the ocean—but not for long. By 4 a.m. the following morning, the authorities mandated an evacuation of their area, Launiupoko. Pamela, the girls, and the cat headed farther out of town over to the Maalaea Harbor. There, they had family friends who owned a boat charter business in a shopping center where they would have cell service. Meanwhile, Keenan waited close to Lahaina to see what happened to their house and neighborhood.

Like refugees, Pamela and the girls arrived safely to Maalaea, along with some other friends of the business owner. Meanwhile, tourists unknowingly came in and out, wondering when their boat tour would embark. Pamela was shocked at the irony of the situation and wondered how the rest of the world could continue as normal.

They waited for Keenan, but Pamela wasn't happy with her husband's decision to stay to see what happened. Luckily, Keenan eventually joined them later that same day. However, Pamela recounts, "Knowing what I know now of similar circumstances that ended up with the loss of separated loved ones, I wouldn't have left without him."

AFTERMATH: HOMELESS BUT NOT HOPELESS

When they finally found safety and cell service, the devastation of Lahaina became clear. Drone footage confirmed what they had feared: Their home was gone. "Our entire neighborhood was reduced to ash," Pamela shared. They narrowly escaped the ground zero of destruction with their lives. Over 2,200 homes were destroyed, leaving more than 12,000 people displaced and approximately one hundred lives lost. At the time, it was the deadliest wildfire in the U.S. and certainly the worst natural disaster in Hawaii's history.

In the days that followed, the Readers stayed with friends. Then they moved into a rental in Kihei on the south side of the island for another week. After outreach to *'ohana* (family in Hawaiian), they were offered a temporary home on Maui by a kind friend, who had a second home on the island. This priceless gift provided much-needed stability. "We were incredibly fortunate," Pamela acknowledged, "but even then, the guilt of having shelter weighed heavily, knowing others were struggling so much more."

For the girls, normalcy returned when school reopened just two weeks later. The private school, Maui Prep, expanded its capacity to accommodate displaced students, creating a sanctuary of routine amidst the upheaval. Keenan even took on the role of volleyball coach, helping his daughters find moments of joy and connection.

Pamela's family eventually purchased a condo in Kaanapali in West Maui as a more permanent home close to the girls' school, as they prepared to rebuild. "We made the decision to stay on Maui," Pamela explained, "not just because it's our home, but because we wanted to be part of Lahaina's rebirth."

LESSONS IN RESILIENCE

The experience taught Pamela profound lessons about preparation and community. She emphasizes the importance of being prepared—both practically and emotionally. "Check your insurance," she advised, half-joking. Their decision to update their coverage two years earlier proved crucial. It enabled them to start rebuilding without financial ruin, albeit nearly two years after the tragedy.

But more than logistics, the kindness of others left the deepest mark. Pamela recalls a stranger who saw her story on the news and sent handmade quilts for her family. Each stitch carried meaning, representing resilience and renewal. One quilt, inspired by sunsets, bore the Phoenix, a symbol of rising from the ashes. "It was the most thoughtful gift we could have received," Pamela said. "It reminded us that even in our lowest of lows, people's kindness can light the way."

Pamela and her family also learned to embrace vulnerability. Accepting help didn't come easily, but it was essential. "I've always been independent," she said, "but this experience taught me it's okay to lean on others. It's okay to ask for help."

THE SPIRIT OF LOOK UP

Amid the chaos, they found moments of beauty and grace. "When you lose everything," Pamela explained, "you realize what truly matters. It's not the things; it's the people, the connections, the memories."

Her family's journey exemplifies the power of perspective. They chose to focus on rebuilding, not just their home but their lives and community. Pamela's involvement in local organizations such as the Na Hale 'O Maui Land Trust and real estate committees, reflects her commitment to creating a stronger future for Lahaina.

Her advice for others is simple yet profound: "Find your community, ask for help, and look for the silver lining, because even in the worst situations, there's always something to be grateful for, so look up."

LAHAINA RISING

Today, Pamela's family is preparing to rebuild their home in Lahaina, embracing the role of pioneers in a community rising from devastation. They plan to return by Thanksgiving 2025, just in time to create new memories in a place they hold dear. "This is our home," she said. "We're not leaving. We're part of its story, and we're here to write the next chapter."

The Reader family's resilience, kindness, and ability to find hope amidst the despair of the Lahaina fire serve as a powerful reminder: Even in the face of unimaginable loss, we can look up, find light, and move forward.

ABOUT PAMELA READER

Originally from New York City, Pamela moved to the Valley Isle in 2001. Nearly twenty-five years later, she and her husband Keenan are raising their two girls on Maui. Pamela is a realtor-broker on Maui with a background in education, and Keenan is a counselor at Maui Prep, where the girls go to school. All are very involved in the community. Pamela volunteers at Maui Prep, is a board member at the Na Hale 'O Maui Land Trust, and co-chairs the Government Affairs Committee in the REALTORS' Association of Maui, a professional trade organization.

To donate to others affected by the Lahaina fire, visit *www.mauiponofoundation.org*. To connect with Pamela, visit *www.PamReader.com*.

LOOK UP – LIFE IS NOW

SAGE ADDERLEY

Life for thirty-nine-year-old Sage was busy, with many moving pieces. Outside of Seattle, Washington, she and her husband Bradley were business owners and involved community members and had three children ages nine, fourteen, and seventeen at home. Like many moms, Sage was juggling a lot of balls. She admitted, "I was trying to do everything—the rat race."

After Sage completed a year-long coaching program, she was invited by her mentor to the Big Island of Hawaii for a celebratory retreat. To encourage Sage to do something for herself, Bradley gifted Sage, coincidentally for her fortieth birthday, roundtrip tickets in September of 2018.

When the time finally came for her trip, Sage kissed Bradley goodbye at the Seattle airport and boarded the six-hour flight.

SUDDEN SHOCK, GUILT, AND GRIEF

Then, in the wee hours of her first night on the Big Island, she was awakened by a phone call. Bradley had had a massive heart attack and had died. Her youngest daughter had found him in his home office that morning as she was getting ready for school.

In utter shock and disbelief, Sage packed up for a return flight home as fast as she could. She hadn't even gotten to say a final goodbye to Bradley. All future plans vanished. She needed to create a new road map for the future.

On the flight and for many months to come, Sage was riddled with guilt. She agonized. "Would things have been different if I had been home?" But unbeknownst to both Sage and Bradley, he had undiagnosed heart disease and an enlarged heart. There was nothing that Sage could have done, but that didn't console her widowed spirit.

During this time of tremendous grief, Sage needed to put her strong, independent, lone wolf personality aside and accept help from others. Neighbors and friends stepped up to the plate. One neighbor set up a meal train. Every night Sage would open the door to another fresh meal for her family from a different community member. Even though she knew she and her kids needed to eat, Sage didn't have the bandwidth to cook. Nor could she bring herself to take on some of the hardest phone calls to Bradley's family, colleagues, and friends. People showed up for Sage and her children, boosting her faith in humanity. Simple items such as surprise bags of kitty litter or fresh roasted coffee on the front door stoop were signs that she wasn't alone.

REBIRTH

By the time Sage turned forty-one, she still felt disconnected from her life. However, she realized she had a choice to make: to stay in that uncomfortable space or do healthy things to work through it. Over the next year, Sage concentrated on creating her own mold. "I get one shot at being Sage," she declared. "I can be who society wants me to be, or I can decide who I am." Her children guided her path. "What do I want my kids to remember me for? Paying bills and working hard or adventures and memories we make together?" she asked herself.

In time, Sage saw Bradley's death as her rebirth. "Suddenly losing someone so close to you is a gigantic reminder of how every moment counts. It's a reminder about what truly matters and to look at where your time and energy are going." The experience reignited her purpose and passion for life.

Since overcoming her tragic loss, Sage has accomplished many things she didn't think a single mother or recent widow could do. For one, she expanded her business. Also, she bought a home. Most importantly, to come full circle, she took all her children on a trip to Hawaii. It was on this trip to the Big Island, outside of Kona in their rental car, that her eldest daughter said, "Mom, this makes me feel like I can do anything in life. You going through everything that you've been through and bringing us here makes me think that anything is possible." From the back seat, Sage's two other kids nodded their heads, sporting sunglasses and living in the now in Hawaii. In reflecting back on this moment, Sage added, "I've done it. Could you give your kids a better gift than that?"

A NEW CHAPTER AND NEW CHALLENGE

After returning to Washington from Hawaii, Sage started another chapter—dating. It didn't take long to meet Jason. Shortly after a few dates, they both decided to be exclusive and not date other people. Within five months, Jason moved in with Sage. It was soon, but life is now; why wait? In hindsight, the move was for a reason.

One month after Jason moved in with Sage, life threw them a curveball. Jason noticed that his neck was swollen and went to the ER. The first doctor thought he had a sinus infection, but Jason still felt like something wasn't right. A couple of days passed, and he returned to the hospital, extremely fatigued and more swollen. He showed another doctor his driver's license as a comparison. This doctor did a scan, finding a tumor the size of a cantaloupe on his heart. He was diagnosed with stage 2 Hodgkin's lymphoma. Almost immediately, Jason started chemotherapy. Just like that, their world shifted. Sage became a full-time caregiver while continuing to be a mom and business owner. Although Sage was not the patient, she shared, "I couldn't believe it. It sounds silly, but I felt cursed. First Bradley. Now Jason."

LOOK UP REMINDER

During this second trying experience, Sage felt as if she was being tested. Had she forgotten how fleeting our time is? Had she been slipping into old habits of being busy and sweating the small stuff such as Amazon orders and to-do lists? It certainly was a reminder to *Look Up*. When asked about her connection to the *Look Up* mantra, she stated, "My story is that. Life is now; be in the moment." She added, "When something devastating happens to you, you have a choice to make. You can sit in the darkness and give up, or you can do your best to find the sliver of light. There is something wonderful on the other side."

After six months of chemotherapy and a month of radiation, Jason is now cancer free and has returned to work, while Sage continues to run her successful business. Sage's three kids aren't kids anymore, but you can bet they're following in her footsteps: *Look Up*. Life is now.

ABOUT SAGE ADDERLEY

Sage Adderley, published author and founder of Tell Your Stories LLC, has over twenty years of experience in creative writing, self-publishing, and community-building. As a high-performance coach for visionary women and a Certified Intentional Creativity Teacher, she blends mindset expertise and compassion to guide creatives from overwhelm to action, helping them write their unique stories and build vibrant communities.

She resides in the magical land of the Pacific Northwest, where she swoons over breathtaking views of Mount Rainier. Sage is a coffee lover and vintage typewriter collector with a passion for kindness and snail-mail.

LIVING WITH GRIEF, BUT SEEING THE BEAUTY

MARY MCQUAIN

After twenty-eight years of service in the United States Navy, Master Chief Mary McQuain found herself stationed at Naval Air Station Lemoore, outside of Fresno, California. It was April of 2020, and she had the opportunity to retire. That year was pivotal for everyone, but drastically so for Mary and her family. At the height of the pandemic, Mary packed up her belongings in California and drove across the country on roads so empty it was eerie. She was enroute to her home in Ohio to join her husband Cecil, a retired senior chief.

Before Mary enlisted in the military at age twenty-one, she had married, and she and her first husband had two daughters, Michelle and Misha. After a messy divorce, Mary decided to take the wise advice of her grandfather. She took the children and joined the Navy. This would ensure a roof over their heads and food on the table.

During her tenure in the U.S. Navy, Mary became part of the military police and was eventually promoted to master chief, one of the Navy's highest accolades. She shared, "It was a man's world. I put on that uniform and I meant business, with no feelings, no compassion." However, it was in the military that she fell in love again. After a handful of years serving, she met Cecil, who also was in the military police. Together they raised four beautiful children—her own two, Michelle and Misha, another daughter, Bonnie Sue, and a son, Calvin, albeit sometimes stationed at different bases depending on the Navy's needs.

BONNIE SUE

In 2020, Bonnie Sue was enrolled in a college close to Mary and Cecil's home. Unlike the rest of the family, Bonnie Sue was blond, blue-eyed, left-handed, and artistic in every way. The others were right-handed and more analytical and had dark hair and eyes. Bonnie Sue was wired differently. She loved animals of every kind and was talented musically. She could play every instrument she picked up—fourteen in total.

Although Mary had just returned to Ohio to join Cecil, for years, they had been fondly thinking of moving to Arizona in retirement. When Bonnie Sue heard about Arizona, she wanted to join them. At that time, she was twenty-two and ready for a change, with a whole life in front of her.

Three days after the dinner conversation about Arizona, Cecil was out of town, having driven to Virginia to pick up their son, who had just returned from deployment. He received a call on his cell phone from their local Ohio police. A young woman, whom the police presumed was Bonnie Sue had overdosed at her home. The only witness was her boyfriend. The body needed to be identified by next of kin. So Mary, after many years of investigating deaths, rapes, and cruelty, needed to do the hardest thing any parent or detective needed to do—identify her deceased daughter.

Because of COVID, everything was difficult, including the investigation, identification of the body, and even holding an intimate service at the crematorium. Pandemic protocol made everything much more painful for families that lost loved ones during this time when visitation and the activities of closure were limited.

Knowing in her gut that Bonnie Sue was not a user of illegal drugs, Mary expanded beyond her military background and consulted a medium. Her motherly instincts were right. The medium told her it had not been an overdose. Bonnie Sue had been slipped some fentanyl and was moved from where it happened to her bed. Mary blamed the boyfriend but couldn't convince the police or anyone else about her gut feeling nor the evidence of a medium.

ARIZONA AND DEEP IN GRIEF

Because of the constant reminders of Bonnie Sue at the house and all around town, Mary and Cecil decided to go ahead and move to Arizona. So, in 2020, they faced the murder of a daughter, retirement, and a move across the country. That was enough for one couple to deal with for countless years, but it was just the beginning of Mary's grief and loss.

Although the move was difficult, it was an escape. However, making the new house feel like home was another story. Mary was so deep in her pain and loss that she wanted to die. For nearly two years, she didn't leave the house. She dedicated herself slavishly to the back and front yard, working innumerable hours in the desert sun. She moved boulders and thorny desert plants that never seemed to let go of the dry dirt, and like the desert plants, the hurt didn't let *her* go either.

MORE LOSSES

Just months after moving to Arizona and less than nine months after Bonnie Sue passed, Mary's first grandson, Jordan, the son of her first daughter, Michelle, contracted COVID. Jordan had diabetes and because of underlying complications, he did not survive. He was only twenty-one years old, and this time the loss hit Mary with double force.

"When your child loses a child and you know what it feels like," explained Mary, "it's absolutely gut-wrenching. It was like I lost Bonnie Sue all over again, plus I felt the pain of my daughter losing her son that I couldn't take away."

After two traumatic losses, Mary threw herself even more into her yardwork. While Mary toiled in the hot desert temperatures and removed thorny plants, Mother Earth was trying to heal her. She was sad and filled with anger at first. Then, as she noticed the transition to beautiful designs in her gardens, she began to smile with awe.

"Bonnie Sue has shown me the beauty I couldn't see before. It's like my serious glasses of the past have been taken off. I feel as if Bonnie Sue is inside me when I'm in the yard. The creative side of me I never had before is coming out."

Throughout the retirement, loss of a daughter and grandson, and the move, Mary's best friend of many decades, Robyn, was by her side. Robyn listened to her and shared talks she had had with Bonnie Sue and Jordan. Robyn let Mary know that Bonnie Sue was okay and at peace, waiting for her. Jordan, too, affirmed through Robyn that he was all right and not to worry. Sadly, Robyn suffered from multiple sclerosis and passed away in her sleep only six months after Jordan had passed.

How can someone come back from three devastating losses in a row? "You never get over losing someone," says Mary. "I'm always in the moment of grief as I walk hand in hand with it daily. The upside is that I now know there's so much more to life and death, as each of these people walk with me daily, giving me signs they are okay."

RETURN TO LIFE

About her connection to the *Look Up* mantra, she comments, "Losing Bonnie Sue, my grandson, and my best friend has taught me through blood, sweat, and tears, that life is worth living. You're going to be sad and mad, and that's okay—but not all the time. Embrace life. Appreciate your time on the planet."

Since that unimaginable year and a half, Mary has continued to landscape and design her entire yard, which has become a Zen garden. With the help of friends, family, neighbors, and non-traditional healthcare practitioners, she is no longer homebound and much stronger psychologically and emotionally. In fact, Mary is sharing with the world some of her recently discovered gifts. She volunteers, working with horses to help children and adolescents with ADHD, ADD, epilepsy, autism, and PTSD.

ABOUT MARY MCQUAIN

Master Chief Master-at-Arms (MACM) Mary Catherine (Pratt) McQuain was born in Parkersburg, West Virginia. She graduated from Marietta High School in 1984, entered the U.S. Naval Reserves in January of 1988, and later went on active duty. She is married to Cecil (retired MACS, U.S.N.), her husband of twenty-nine years, and they have four children as well as seven grandchildren. Mary now teaches Horse Powered Reading and volunteers with the horses and donkeys at Mighty Minds in Arizona.

ALMOST GONE WITH THE WIND – HURRICANE ANDREW

THE MCCOMBS

In late August of 1992, it was a typical South Florida summer week for the McCombs. John and Barb had recently moved to Kendall, a western suburb of Miami, and both worked full time. John had a job as an electrical engineer at a local electrical utility company, while Barb worked from home for a technology headhunter in Ohio, their former home state. This allowed Barb time to look after their daughter Beth, who was entering middle school. To combat the heat and relax from the grind, all enjoyed the backyard pool and watersports, especially their ski boat and SCUBA diving.

WEATHER REPORT

This week, Barb had been paying attention to Bryan Norcross, Channel 4's weatherman, about another developing tropical depression. By Saturday afternoon, a storm named Andrew appeared to be on a path toward South Florida. In a late afternoon breaking update, Norcross advised that South Florida was going to be hit, although exactly where and how hard, no one knew. However, the time to prepare was then, before the anticipated hit early morning Monday, August 24.

With only thirty-six hours to get ready, when John and Barb's sister Janine got home from SCUBA diving in the Keys, Barb immediately gave them the update. Janine stayed with Beth while John went to Home Depot and Barb went to Publix, the grocery store. It was 8:30 p.m., and Publix was more crowded than during the holidays or for the Superbowl. Every checkout was open, with lines twenty or more people deep. The store's shelves had already been picked clean, and only a few, mostly defective, canned goods were left. After nearly an hour, Barb returned home with a few provisions to find John empty-handed. No plywood remained at Home Depot to secure windows.

PREPARATION FOR THE STORM

The next day they made a nonstop effort to prepare. John tried two other Home Depots at the crack of dawn, but both had lines out the door. Instead of wasting several hours in line, he decided to come home and make do with what they already had.

By 8 a.m., the weather center had issued an evacuation order for all the Keys. Janine had spent the night, as the plan was to finish her dive certification that Sunday. Not yet aware of the latest news, she picked up the phone to call the dive instructor to see if class was still on. Barb shared, "We had a good laugh over that. Here all the Keys are heading for cover, and Janine's wondering if her dive class is still on!" Learning this, Janine wanted to head to her apartment, just a half-hour north in Broward County. However, the latest update predicted that Broward would get the brunt of the storm and the area wouldn't be safe. John and Barb wouldn't hear of Janine leaving, fearing she'd be stranded in the evacuation traffic. So Janine stayed.

The next-door neighbors had already prepared and had shutters on all their windows. Their neighbor Martin, his brother Chris, and their two boys, spent the morning with John taking down the McComb's decorative shutters and screwing them directly over the windows. However, that left six-inch gaps. Janine and Barb found scraps of wood by yanking off shelves from the storage room as well as repurposing Beth's bedroom closet doors. John nailed the random strips of plywood over the still-exposed windows. When every window was covered, John removed the

TV antenna and tied down their two boats to a large palm tree and fence posts.

Around 7 p.m., the day began to look eerie, with heavy clouds and light rain. Everyone finished outside and John headed inside where even more prep awaited. The group located supplies and equipment: propane, camping stove, lantern, wooden matches, an aluminum coffeepot, and a small, battery-powered black-and-white TV. While Beth and Janine filled saved gallon milk jugs with water, Barb brewed a large pot of coffee and put it in a thermos to keep with them during the storm.

With everything prepped, everyone took showers. Then, they scrubbed the tubs and filled them with fresh water for flushing toilets if the water system failed. Thoroughly exhausted, they settled in the family room to listen to ongoing weather reports. The updates had changed, predicting Andrew's sure hit to at least part of Dade County.

HUNKERING DOWN

By 3:30 a.m., Norcross and his team at Channel 4 had moved from the news desk to a corridor in the interior of the station. Shortly thereafter, the McCombs lost power and the wind picked up. Everyone, including the dog and cat, moved into the master bathroom with cushions, sleeping blankets, pillows, a lantern, the battery-powered TV, and a thermos of coffee. The storm was anticipated to hit in an hour.

Almost instantly, the winds grew more intense. "It truly sounded like the closest thing to being bombed that I could ever imagine," commented Barb. As the master bathroom had an exterior door out to the lanai, Barb suggested moving into the inner hallway, which had a walk-in closet across from the bathroom. John got the mattress from the bed to make a fourth wall to close in the hallway in case the bedroom windows blew in. It was a tight space, only big enough for the four of them seated crossed-legged and their pets curled in the corners.

Just then, they heard one of the windows blow out in the living or dining room. Even though they were behind a closed door, little drops of water began to fall on them. All envisioned the roof torn away and a miniature tornado on the other side of the door. They didn't know it at the time, but the storm had once again shifted, and they were in the strongest part of the hurricane, in line with the north wall of the eye.

At this point, Barb expected John to make some silly remark to ease the tension, but she looked at him and saw no expression. He was looking up in concentration. In this moment, Barb realized their lives were possibly in danger. All they could do was stay put and wait.

Gradually, over the hours, the strongest winds subsided, but without electricity and with all the windows boarded up, it was mighty hot. The tile floor was the best bet for a cool space to sack out, so they attempted to sleep for a bit.

THE AFTERMATH

After the fury of Andrew, around 8 a.m. on Monday, it was light out and the winds were manageable. John and Barb emerged to check out the damage that had been done, not only to their own home but the neighborhood. The screened enclosure over their pool had been torn apart, with the support beams crisscrossed every which way across the pool and roof. Their neighbors' giant Norfolk pine had fallen across the fence, just missing the McCombs' bedroom where they were all hunkered down. The entire yard was virtually covered with broken ceramic roof tiles, shingles, plywood, tar paper, and mounds of shrubs and tree debris. Inside the house everything was covered in a film of water, dirt, and leaves that had been forced in through the broken window and a gap in Barb's office window.

Like the McCombs, the neighbors started coming out little by little Monday mid-morning. Many found themselves trying to hold back tears. The scene was overwhelming, like the aftermath of a bomb attack.

Although the fear of the storm, its damage, and possible death were terrifying, the next weeks or months were the most trying times for the McCombs and the South Florida community. Barb salvaged what she could and set up a makeshift camp on their back porch. She put up a portable table with a propane stove, lantern, and grill. Barb stressed, "I felt like we were wilderness camping in a landfill."

RECOVERING

For the remainder of the recovery process, John worked seven days a week dawn to dusk with the electric company's round-the-clock restoration efforts. Nightly, John and Barb would put together a to-do list for Barb to complete the following day. However, the list never seemed to get accomplished in terms of getting the house back in order. Many things had to be done right in the moment to be able to live. When the water came on three days after the storm, the priority was washing laundry by hand and hanging it out to dry across the patio.

During the first few days, an ongoing task for Barb, Janine, and Beth was cleaning up the debris in the yard so they could get Janine's car and Barb's van out of the backyard. They had parked them there for protection, but both windshields had been shattered. The biggest concern was to avoid getting a flat as they drove the vehicles over the lawn. By Wednesday, Janine headed up the turnpike to check on her apartment, which fortunately hadn't been touched. Thus, she focused her efforts on picking up supplies for John and Barb, most importantly a generator.

On day five, Janine brought them the new generator, which John rigged up to share with the neighbors. It was a gas generator and noisy, but it enabled them to use their TV, lights, refrigerator, and fans at night. Even with the generator, the McCombs couldn't use their electric stove, oven, or Barb's computer until the main power came on three weeks later in mid-September.

During the first several weeks, the noise was relentless. Twenty-four seven they heard the generators, chainsaws, and military aircraft from the nearby airport. However, no one had a hard time sleeping. The combination of ninety-five-degree heat and hard work knocked them right out despite the constant sound of the generator.

Although the McCombs suffered damage to their home, they were lucky to have an intact roof and three bedrooms to sleep in. Other neighbors weren't so fortunate. Many lost entire roofs and garages. They were forced to find refuge with family and/or friends in Broward and West Palm Beach Counties. Others wanted to stay close to their homes during the rebuild; thus, it was common to find RVs and campers parked on the neighborhood lawns.

One of the *Look Up* components of Andrew was its profound impact on camaraderie. Typically, South Floridians spend summer inside with AC. After Andrew, everyone was living in their backyards. Everyone pooled every resource they had to help out one another and the group, sharing chainsaws, generators, and more.

With John's expertise, he found himself giving a hand to neighbors with various power problems or correcting potential safety hazards. Likewise, a neighborly nurse gave Barb a tetanus shot after she stepped on a roofing nail. Barb repaid the favor with a daily thermos of hot coffee for the nurse and her family.

In mid-September, Beth went back to school and Barb went back to work. However, throughout the fall of 1992, things weren't normal in their neighborhood or Dade County. With so many displaced families leaving their homes and neighborhoods without power, a curfew was in place. The presence of the National Guard was prevalent throughout September and October to prevent looting.

Outside of curfew hours, it was construction time every day. The continuous droning of dump trucks, beeping when they backed up, and the annoying jingles of the food trucks (aka "roach coaches") was unyielding. Barb tried to drown it all out and work but said, "I thought I was going to develop a nervous tic from having to listen to it."

By the end of 1992, the McComb's roof had been retiled. The new footers had been poured for the large screen enclosure for the pool, which they built themselves. Likewise, the neighbors' homes were revitalized for the holidays and the New Year celebrations.

Beth, at the time thirteen, came up with a cute Hurricane Andrew version of the "Twelve Days of Christmas." Here's a taste of it:

"On the 24th of August, Andrew gave to me . . .
my neighbors' shingles in my palm tree. . . ."

LOOKING UP

In looking back on it, Barb observed, "After two years of living in Miami and feeling somewhat like outsiders, it became truly home. Andrew was a bonding moment for the area. I realized

how we are all connected. We got to know our neighbors."
Many from Miami-Dade who lived through Andrew say there's
a pre-Andrew and a post-Andrew mentality. When asked
about this and her connection to *Look Up,* Barb shared, "Fond
memories with neighbors and friends quickly overshadowed all
the sadness and frustration of the earliest weeks following the
storm. This helped to keep us on a mentally positive path back
to normalcy." The McCombs found the upside of the Great
Hurricane of 1992 and called Miami home for another twenty-
three years.

ABOUT THE MCCOMBS

John and Barb McComb now live in rural Oklahoma to
be close to family, but they still consider Miami home.
Both are happily retired and enjoy walks among their
large oak trees. Beth is now grown and forging her own
path. She's a helicopter pilot who loves to SCUBA dive
and spend time with her husband and helicopter pilot
Shay and their dog Tucker at their North Carolina home.

THE TIDAL WAVE OF LOSS

AMY BECKER

In the early 2020s, the Beckers were a family of four living in a small town in western Wisconsin. Both Marty and Amy grew up in the area and had dreamed of having a nice home, a family, and jobs not far from their families. Marty, a local contractor, built homes with pride, and in his free time, he played fastpitch softball. Amy, a clinical manager in Pediatrics at a La Crosse area hospital, balanced her demanding job with a passion for endurance sports. She ran, biked, or swam, competing in marathons and triathlons, including two full IRONMAN triathlons.

The Beckers' oldest daughter, Sydney, grew up in the area, but after graduating from high school, she moved across the state to

Milwaukee. Because of COVID-19, Sydney took a break from attending the University of Wisconsin–Milwaukee and worked at a local café, living with her boyfriend. She planned to return to UW–Milwaukee when she could. Meanwhile, the younger of the two daughters, Claire, was still in high school, involved in student council and many sports. Claire, like her older sister and parents, excelled athletically. Both sisters, like their mother, were exceptional runners, both in track and field and cross-country.

Every summer, the Beckers escaped to Hayward, Wisconsin, where they relished the "Up North" lifestyle of fishing, tubing, and waterskiing. But the summer of 2022 was different. Claire had qualified for the state track meet, a momentous event that could pave the way for a collegiate running career. The night before the race, the family slept with dreams of victory. Sydney was set to join them the next morning.

THE UNTHINKABLE

In the middle of the night, Amy was awakened by the doorbell. She nervously wondered why anyone would be at their house so late, so she nudged Marty. He answered the door to face two grim-looking police officers. They verified Marty's name and asked if he was Sydney Becker's father. When he replied that he was, they notified both Marty and Amy, who had joined him, that Sydney had died.

Amy's legs buckled and she collapsed to the floor, a guttural scream escaping her lips. "No! No! This can't be happening! It can't be true!" She and Marty were expecting to see Sydney the very next morning to cheer on Claire. Now the world had turned upside down. All they could do was cling to each other, desperate for more details and the reason for this incomprehensible tragedy. The officers gave Marty the number for the medical examiner and respectfully left.

Marty and Amy immediately called the medical examiner, and he told them Sydney had taken her own life and her boyfriend had found her. The medical examiner explained how they were going to handle her body and get her to a local funeral home in Galesville early the next day. The weight of guilt and despair crushed the two parents. To make matters worse, they were paralyzed by the agonizing decision of when to tell Claire.

Shortly after the call with the examiner, they called the detective. She told the Beckers that Sydney and her boyfriend had been in a fight, and that the boyfriend had left to go to the local convenience store when Sydney made her decision. "I heard bits and pieces," said Amy, "but nothing was registering or sinking in at all. I just paced and cried constantly."

When Claire awoke at a normal time to catch the school bus at 7 a.m., Marty and Amy still didn't know what to do. Should they tell her now or after the meet? They didn't want her running career to be ruined for life, so they decided to stay strong, stoic, and silent with the heartbreaking secret.

Marty had to leave when Claire got up. He knew all too well that he couldn't look at her and keep it together. He went straight to his parents' home to tell them the horrific news. When Claire was out of the house, Amy made some of the most difficult phone calls of her life to her sister and parents. Phones were dropped and people cried at the painful news. Both Marty and Amy asked all family members not to say anything to Claire, as most would be attending the race.

THE TRACK MEET

At the track meet, Amy, Marty, and all family members wore sunglasses to hide that they'd been crying all morning. It was surely a testament to the family's love and togetherness. Before the race, Claire asked her mom multiple times about Sydney. Eventually, Amy told her Sydney had gotten into a fight with her boyfriend and wasn't going to make it. "It was hell to hold it back from her," Amy shared. "All I wanted to do was jump off the high bleachers." When Claire was not competing, Marty had to go for a walk and sit in his truck to shelter his emotions.

Claire's race was successful. She ranked tenth in the 3200-meter run (the "two-mile"), with her best time. She finished thirteenth at the state meet, which would be enough to vie for a scholarship to Wisconsin and Minnesota state universities. To celebrate, she wanted to go for ice cream. Despite the terrible secret, Marty and Amy joined her—another act of holding it together for the family. However, when the Beckers arrived home, Claire had had enough and demanded, "Okay, where is Sydney?"

THE AGONIZING REALITY

Marty and Amy sat Claire down on the couch and told her that Sydney was no longer alive. Claire wailed uncontrollably in pure agony. She ran outside into the dark, her screams piercing the night. Bolting as far from the house as she could, she finally dropped, her grief too immense to contain.

Finally, Amy and Marty got Claire to return to the house, where she started to vomit from her flood of emotions. All three ended up sleeping on the living room floor, clinging to one another. Both parents were afraid to leave Claire alone.

In the following days, they made necessary arrangements in a state of numb disbelief. The first blow was seeing Sydney's body on the steel table covered with a paper cloth, a moment of agonizing reality for Amy and Marty. "We cried in disbelief and kissed her all over her face," said Amy. When the funeral director went about his job in a nonchalant way, quickly moving to the selection of Sydney's coffin, Amy exploded. "This is *stupid!* I should be helping her pick out her *wedding dress,* not her coffin!" All the excruciating decisions the couple needed to make so fast when they were so fragile felt to them like pounding ocean waves in a relentless storm.

The wake became the next set of waves. The Beckers met it with a deceptive sense of comfort and dazed exhaustion. Surrounded by both familiar and unfamiliar people, it was too much too soon. However, the following day of the funeral brought the finality of it all to a crescendo. At the service, Amy, Marty, and Claire saw Sydney's face for the last time. Although Sydney's friends shared tributes at the service, which brought solace, it was all too much anguish to bear. The funeral director advised that the three leave when the casket was closed.

The customary post-funeral meal and visit at the North Bend Lions Club felt like a cruel ritual for the family just starting to grieve. "Food? Not interested at all!" expressed Amy later. "I was just pacing, confused, and sad. How could others eat at this time?" For quite a while afterward, supportive family and friends had to remind the Beckers to eat, let alone sleep.

The very next day, Amy visited the cemetery and witnessed the outline of the freshly tilled earth. "I wanted to die and thought about unburying her and taking Sydney home," she shared. "It sounds crazy, but a mother's brain does funny things." Probably the most helpful occurrence that day was a good friend kindly bringing the plants and flowers from the service to their home. This grounded Amy. Right then and there, she was bound to keep them alive in memory of Sydney. Since then, Amy has designed two gardens in Sydney's honor—one in the backyard and one at the mailbox. Gardening has helped her cope. She added that "exercise, counseling, and doing things that make me feel more connected to Sydney also helped, such as getting a dragonfly tattoo in her memory and a nose piercing just like she had."

That said, Amy admits, "We have nowhere near overcome this, but Marty and I need to stay on Earth for our Claire Bear." Amy looks for Sydney every day, wondering where she is. In heaven? And with whom?

DEALING WITH GRIEF AND HELPING OTHERS

Both Amy and Marty have returned to work, and the Beckers continue to go Up North for summer vacations to fish, tube, and ski. Amy admits her story connects to the *Look Up* mantra because, "Life is short. You must live in the moment." She adds, "It's healing to talk about Sydney. In fact, I teach at a local healthcare facility, and when I speak of suicide, I share her story. If there's an upside, it's that I can help build awareness that suicide is not a selfish act. It's a mental illness—depression and anxiety."

To honor Sydney and further build awareness around mental health, in September of 2023, the Mini Donut Foundation's half-marathon and 5K run/walk and kids' race were dedicated to Sydney Becker. Over five hundred runners and walkers were in attendance. The Beckers ran in the Mini Donut Foundation's race in 2023 and are still involved, intending to run the race every September.

To further give back to their community, the Beckers annually award a local high school outstanding runner/athlete the Sydney Becker Memorial Scholarship. It's a tribute to Sydney's legacy and a testament to the strength of a family that refused to be broken.

When asked what advice Amy would give to someone going through a similar situation, she offered this wise guidance: "Get counseling early, talk about it, and don't listen to the clichés that tell you there are something like five stages of grief and then you'll be in a better place. That advice is more for loved ones of people who are actively dying. It's not for those who have lost someone too early or unexpectedly to suicide."

Just as the ocean ebbs and flows, so does grief and the feeling of loss. For the Beckers, sometimes days come with just a few rough waves and others bring a tidal wave, leaving them and others breathless. However, together the Beckers, along with a strong community of friends, family, and colleagues, are navigating the waves and making it safely ashore. They're encouraging everyone to keep going and keep looking up, because life, with all its pain and joy, is still worth living.

ABOUT AMY BECKER

Amy is a proud mother, wife, and athlete, and the Lead Educator in the Quality & Patient Safety Department at Emplify Health, previously known as Gundersen Health System, in La Crosse, Wisconsin. She and Marty are excited to see their daughter Claire attend the University of Minnesota at Duluth and spend some quality time Up North. All three actively support the Mini Donut Foundation *(www.minidonutfoundation.com)* as well as the Sydney Becker Scholarship Fund.

PART 2:

THE COURAGE TO RESTART

STARTING OVER, NOT ONCE BUT TWICE

CHONG HANG

In a rural village in Laos, the Hangs were Hmong farmers with four children. Chong was the eldest boy with a younger brother, Pao, and two sisters, Sophie and Mee. Witnessing how hard his father and mother worked in the fields, Chong dreamed of going to school and getting a higher education. However, the closest boarding school was an hour away by plane. Fortunately, when he was only eight years old, Chong was the only kid selected from his town of Bokeo to attend that Catholic boarding school. His dream came true in 1971, but only for a few years. The Vietnam War broke out, forcing the school to close and Chong to return to his village.

Chong's homecoming was not sweet—in fact, quite the opposite. He shared that upon arriving at his village, "No one came to greet me as they normally would, and the once bustling community was now a ghost town." Many families had already fled into the jungles. In fact, his brother and two sisters had already left for Thailand, but steadfast, Chong's parents had waited for his return from school. Every night, communist soldiers enforced curfews and patrolled their homes to make sure no one else fled. Just after dusk, only a day after Chong returned home, his mother ordered him to pack essentials because they would cross the Mekong River to safety in Thailand that night.

Chong didn't ask any questions and quickly packed two pairs of clothes and one pair of shoes in a backpack. His father had prearranged an escape by boat with a trusted local; however, they needed to walk for an hour to meet the boat. At midnight, they fled the village, risking their lives, hoping the soldiers would be asleep. Through the dark jungle, they arrived at the Mekong River and boarded the boat. The risk was worth it. Every member of the family was now out of Laos. With the help of family friends, all six family members were safely and happily reunited in Thailand. For the next six months, they lived illegally with local residents and helped them farm until the Thai government and the United Nations created an official refugee site in 1975.

BECOMING REFUGEES IN THAILAND

Adapting to a new life in a new country at the age of twelve was frustrating for Chong to say the least. For the next five years, he and his family were sealed off from the rest of the world. They lived behind barbed wire fences in Ban Tong with another approximately seven thousand Hmong refugees. Once again, Chong threw himself into school, learning three new languages: Thai, English, and French. While at Ban Tong, he heard endless chatter among the elders about where they'd continue their lives. Many talked of Australia, Germany, and France, but the most desirable of all was the United States.

One by one, other families were deployed to foreign places, with priority given to those who had worked for the CIA or fought in the war. As the Hangs were farmers, they waited and waited for their opportunity. During this time in Ban Tong, both Sophie and Mee met their husbands. Sophie safely moved to France. Mee met a Thai man and married, staying legally in Thailand. However, the sisters weren't the only ones who fell in love in Ban Tong. At school, Chong was introduced to Boua. Almost instantly, they bonded. Boua and Chong would go to school and water the garden together. In October of 1978, they were married at the camp, ensuring that when they had their turn to emigrate, Boua and Chong would start a new life together in a new country.

AMERICA AND MORE ADJUSTMENT

In 1980, the Hangs' luck turned with the help of an American sponsor. The Siefkas family in Galesville, Wisconsin, agreed to house and assist the Hang family of five in adapting to a new culture. Jim, Jackie, and their four-year-old daughter Heidi welcomed Chong's family, including his parents, his younger brother, Pao, himself and Boua, into their rural farmhouse. At the time, Jim was a professor at the University of Wisconsin–La Crosse. Every morning, he dropped them off at the college to learn English and picked them up after work. On the weekends, Jackie taught the Hangs how to count quarters, nickels, and dimes that make up a U.S. dollar. However, the Hangs had some things to teach the Siefkas family, too. As Chong was the best English speaker, he was the interpreter most of the time. However, actions can speak louder than words.

One of the first mornings at the house, Chong's mother stood in front of the stove. She wanted to cook for everyone. Jackie instructed her how to turn the stove on and off. Mrs. Hang cooked a Hmong staple, white rice and a stir fry. Afterward, the Hangs indicated they wanted to go to the grocery store. While in the store, the father picked up a handful of the hottest chili peppers available. Both Jim and Jackie tried to explain that the peppers were too hot, but the father simply nodded his head. The next meal prepared by Mrs. Hang included more spice. Once again without words, Mr. Hang showed Jim how to be a man by eating an entire pepper. Not accustomed to hot and spicy foods, Jim attempted to eat just a small bite. The father was proud to show off his manhood, culture, and bravery. Jim laughed it off while wiping sweat from his brow and eating some white rice.

The Hangs spent two months in Galesville—a few weeks with the Siefkas family and the rest in an apartment off Main Street, close to the hardware, grocery, and furniture stores. They were the only Asian family in town, but they experienced no prejudice. People were quite friendly and accommodating. In fact, Jim helped Chong's father get a job at the local furniture store. Although Mr. Hang didn't speak English, the owner could use him for odd jobs and cleaning. One day, early on at the store, the owner announced, "Break time," but Mr. Hang continued to work. The next day, the owner asked Chong to translate for his father, but he didn't understand break time either—until the owner explained to Chong that a break means to stop working. Jim, the owner, Chong, and his father had a chuckle about the lost-in-translation moment.

SCHOOL AND A GROWING FAMILY

With relatives in the Seattle area, the Hangs decided to relocate to the Pacific Northwest. There, the younger Hmong immigrants, along with Chong, enrolled in public school for the first time. Unlike in the Midwest, they were harassed daily. They attempted to ignore the name calling and prodding, but events escalated and evolved into brawls on the school buses, in the cafeteria, and on the soccer fields.

To make life even more challenging, Boua and Chong welcomed their first child, a boy. Meanwhile, after school and on the weekends, Chong was working multiple odd jobs for meager wages. Even with an infant at home as well as school and work, Chong managed to finish high school. He then moved with his family to Redding, California, for college.

In California, Chong's family grew significantly to eight children. They struggled to make ends meet, but Chong was convinced that getting a bachelor's degree was the only way out of poverty. In 1993, he graduated with a degree in industrial engineering. Shortly thereafter, Chong and his family moved to Charlotte, North Carolina, where they continued to climb the social ladder.

LIVING THE AMERICAN DREAM

When recounting his journey, Chong shared, "I was forced to start over not once but twice. Instead of falling victim to my circumstances each time, I chose to press forward. I never complained. I always looked up." In 2015, Chong took a pilgrimage to his hometown in Laos. His home and neighborhood were no longer there. The area had been taken over by banana plantations. Also, he returned to his former school. It was still standing and operating as a school, but with a changed name. Chong had come full circle, completing his original dream of being educated and so much more.

Chong is living his version of the American dream. "I have all the things I need," he affirms. "I have had many opportunities. I have eight children and sixteen grandchildren. All my kids are college educated and living their own version of the American dream."

ABOUT CHONG HANG

Chong Hang is a proud family man and a professional, with humble beginnings in Laos. Chong shares his family's powerful journey because the story of Hmong immigrants is not often told. He hopes this inspires others to remain persistent no matter what their journey entails.

POST-TRAUMATIC TRANSFORMATION

HELENA SUMMER

In late summer of 1991 in the Croatian part of Yugoslavia, Helena was just a teenager when her mother firmly instructed, "Look at the house as if you may never see it again. Pack a bag. Take only what you must have!" Although the temperatures were still balmy, Helena rushed to grab a blanket, letters from a boy she had a crush on, and three special books.

At the time, the Yugoslavian National Army was attacking its own state, Croatia. As the Croatian Independence War approached their hometown of Osijek, Helena and her mother sought protection in a neighbor's little underground garage. They shared this makeshift bomb shelter with three other families whose homes didn't have any underground protection.

Earlier that summer, as the rumors of a war breaking out became more intense, many Croatian schools partnered with schools abroad to have them take in students before the school year started. Fortunately, Helena's twin sister went with her classmates to Hungary, escaping the war entirely. However, the rest of the family was not so lucky. Helena's nineteen-year-old brother was sent to the front lines to fight. Unlike her twin, Helena attended a different school that did not secure a sister school abroad. She and her mother would have to be brave and ride out the war.

SURVIVING WAR

On their first days in the bomb shelter, they heard the war in the distance. Helena shares, "We heard planes. Bombs were dropping. It was like living in a movie, not real life." However, it quickly became reality, which was not Hollywoodized. At times, Helena and the others had to hunker down in the shelter for fifty or more continuous hours as the Yugoslavian army's planes attacked the surrounding area. When the bombings let up, everyone played a part in surviving— finding food and helping one another. At only sixteen, Helena was quickly trained to be in the first aid group, caring for wounded civilians, which meant witnessing the worst.

In the evenings, the families would listen to a transistor radio for news of the war, but also of the recent deaths. "We became numb to the deaths," said Helena. "Every day someone died that we knew. Our own military was killing our people." To escape the chaos of wartime as well as the tensions inside the shelter, Helena turned to her books, one of which was a meditation book. The book instructed readers on how to meditate, paying attention to your breath, and being in the moment for twenty minutes, twice a day. Helena said, "War puts you into this very moment for survival. If you don't find an upside and *Look Up,* you develop PTSD. If you're able to find the upside, you develop post-traumatic transformation."

Under communist rule in Yugoslavia, meditation topics were forbidden, but that book was a way for Helena to triumph over the war and her turbulent childhood. Although the war was hell, her earlier childhood was filled with fear, violence, and pain as well. Her parents had a volatile relationship. Helena's father was physically abusive to her mother and all the kids. He would threaten to kill them and gave each of them vulgar nicknames, such as Helena's, "Little Slut." All feared for their lives with him around. A year before the war, her mother finally left and divorced him. As Helena recounts, "One hell was over, but then another one began."

THE SOLACE OF MEDITATION

During this survival mode stage of the war, the tiny underground garage served as a safe zone for the body, but Helena's mind needed something more. It needed peace. Helena prayed for it and the door opened. A friend who was a practitioner of Maharishi's Transcendental Meditation (TM) took Helena under her wing. She introduced her to TM teachers who took sympathy on her and initiated her into the process. She was the youngest student they'd ever had.

Numerous studies on meditation had shown that if one percent of the population meditated, crime levels improved. Therefore, the TM group organized a month-long peace-creation meditation retreat in Pula, a town on the northwest coast of Croatia, away from the warzone. Without a foreign school option and with war at her doorstep, Helena accepted the invitation. She said goodbye to her mother and headed to Pula, hoping to stop the war with her faith and dedication. Little did she know that her life would again drastically change.

As if she were in a bubble of positivity, away from her troubled past, escaping the war and her uncertain future, that retreat fortified her trust in meditation and the power of perspective. But alas! The month ended and where was Helena to go? She couldn't go home as her city was occupied. In fact, the train tracks leading to Osijek had been destroyed by bombings. With no identification, no money, and only the clothes she packed from home, her sole option was a refugee center nearby. Immediately, Helena knew she didn't fit in, but she had no choice. Unlike Helena, who had left her home before it was occupied, the others had run for their lives, witnessing rape and murder. Everyone at the refugee camp was a victim. It was a sad and painful place to be.

After nearly three months at the camp, Helena awoke one night to the sound of a young woman weeping uncontrollably. It was something more painful and gut-wrenching than anything she had heard before. The young woman's baby had died that night, freezing to death. The following morning Helena heard the camp's rumor mill blaming the mother for not covering the baby more sufficiently. Helena couldn't stand it anymore. "There was no compassion at the camp. I got mad at God. So, I ran away from the refugee camp to find God and kick his butt. I was an enraged sixteen-year-old!"

SEARCHING FOR GOD

She fled the refugee camp, determined to find God. She didn't know if she should turn left or right, but she asked everyone she met: "Excuse me, where is God?" People replied, "in the church," "in the Bible," "in nature," "in your heart," "everywhere." It was getting late and cold, but she didn't give up.

Whether it was simply being at the right place at the right time or due to her internal compass, Helena came across three glowing women. They had beautiful faces with round, pink cheeks. After months of being surrounded by refugees, all with sharp lines of worry on their faces and almost a grey hue to their complexions, these three women appeared angelic. Helena inquired, "Where is God?"

"Why do you ask us?" they replied.

Helena responded, "I don't know. You're not special. I ask this of everyone." They smiled and said, "Come with us." They were nuns.

Although it took time and study, Helena became a nun. She vowed to honor celibacy, simplicity, and poverty. She felt safe and protected by her new family. With their support, she finished high school. Also, she became a missionary, traveling to Germany, Austria, and Switzerland, which opened her eyes to the world and other cultures. This was absolutely the most magical time of her life: simple living and high thinking. It was all about service, prayer, and surrender. However, at the age of twenty-one and after six years as a nun, Helena's hormones kicked in. She wondered what a hug or a first kiss felt like and realized she couldn't observe her vow of celibacy anymore. She left, and her nun family shunned her. By that time, the war was over, so Helena headed for home to be with her mother, who luckily had survived the occupation of their town.

FROM NUN TO WIFE

She returned home a changed woman, but rather naïve. She didn't know much about normal life, pop culture, or even money. She certainly didn't know about romance. Her mother, very traditional, commented, "I'm scared for you. You don't have a man, but you are so different now that a regular guy would take advantage of you."

Helena was at a turning point—no longer a nun and looking for love, for the right man. Somewhat serendipitously, Helena received a call from a friend she'd known during her missionary years. He told her a Slovenian priest had left the church. "You left. Primus left. You two should just marry," he urged Helena.

The two knew of each other through the church circle and newsletters, but they had never met. However, after a friendly phone call, they decided to meet.

Primus took a train to Helena's hometown, and for their first date, they sat on a bench by the river. They were both so awkward at first, they didn't even look at each other, but eventually they discussed their similarities and getting married. They both loved the simple life a spiritual path provides; so, they married shortly thereafter and kept all the other vows of the church minus celibacy.

Like many newlyweds then or now, Helena and Primus were broke. They lived with their parents, both in Slovenia and Croatia. Eventually, they purchased a minivan to live in and made money by buying and selling jars of honey and handpicked tea door to door. Even with a modest lifestyle, they were able to save money to go on pilgrimages to India and Japan.

After many good times, travels, and seven years together, not only was Primus's health declining with asthma and a skin ailment, but Helena started to experience breathing problems when sleeping. These physical signs coupled with a vivid dream led Primus and Helena to divorce, promising to be forever friends.

MORE TURNOVER AND A NEW CAREER

Still caring for Helena and wanting to help her in her next chapter of life, Primus went so far as to go online and find a single, successful businessman in Hawaii who was a cross between Tom Cruise and Mel Gibson. Primus started the online conversation with Toby and passed it off to Helena to continue. Fast forward to 2004, and the two met in London. On day three, Toby proposed to Helena by whispering to her on the bus. She said yes. Both returned to their respective homes with plans for Toby to travel to Croatia where they would marry. Together, they were then able to get a visa for Helena to travel to Hawaii.

In the States, Helena was challenged with reinventing herself once again. Her first husband continued to be her sounding board, suggesting, "The upside is you get to live in Hawaii, learn to surf, and improve your English. Learn to have fun and live a little!" Although living in paradise had its ups, it also had its downs. It was in Hawaii that Helena embarked on her business as a life and love coach, which she continues today. However, her marriage was not the right match. She found herself at another crossroads, divorced again at the age of thirty.

During this post-divorce time, Helena remembers a highly influential conversation with her cousin, who said, "You are in the best part of life. You have a career. You're in Hawaii. You can date men ten years younger or older. The world is your oyster." This conversation was the fuel for a Herculean goal of finding out what makes men tick. At its heart, she wanted to learn how to respect them after her painful past with her father and two divorces in hopes of turning that wisdom into a career.

Helena reveals her multiple connections throughout her life's journey to the *Look Up* mantra: "It works in every area of our lives, even in war. The world would be a much better place if people knew that looking up is available to them. I'm happy to report," she added, "that I was able to look up and experience post-traumatic *transformation,* when I could have expected post-traumatic stress disorder."

Fast forward to present, and Helena lives in Austin, Texas, with her loving husband Lexi. Professionally, Helena helps high achievers in their romantic lives. She explains, "Lexi and I have a very peaceful and playful marriage. We have harmony. I teach other people how to have a peaceful and playful marriage with my programs."

ABOUT HELENA SUMMER

Helena Summer is a master love coach, award-winning speaker, and relationship educator with over two decades of international experience. She has worked with clients on every continent, has led a TV show, and was featured as an expert in a movie about energy psychology. She has personally planted 166 trees. In her ideal world, she would live with one foot in stilettos and the other foot in the mud. To connect with Helena and learn more about her upcoming book, visit *www.helenasummer.com.*

RISKING ALL AND BRAVING 7,000 MILES FOR A DREAM

CRISTINA AND EMILY RODRIGUEZ

Cristina was born and raised in Santiago de Cuba, a city of 550,000 people, in the eastern portion of Cuba called El Oriente. She lived in a cement high-rise in an apartment she shared with her parents, five siblings, and extended family. With only three bedrooms and one bathroom, it was quite tight. In time, her siblings married and moved elsewhere with their families, but Cristina stayed, as she was the youngest.

She completed a college degree in English in 1994 in the hope of one day moving to the United States. However, in the '90s, Cuba's economy was quite unstable without the U.S.S.R.'s financial support. In fact, the era was deemed "the Special Period," similar to the Great Depression era. This left Cristina with few career options. With her linguistic ability, she found her first job, albeit far from her home, at the Bacardi Museum as a tour guide. Four years later, with the help of a friend, she landed a job closer to her home as a tour guide at the Santa Ifigenia Cemetery. "At first, it was so sad, I thought I'd go crazy," she recalled. "But I started to see it as a museum and fell in love with its stories." Santa Ifigenia Cemetery is the resting place of many famous figures such as Carlos Manuel de Céspedes (1874), José Martí (1895), Compay Segundo (2003), and Fidel Castro (2016).

In 2003, Cristina and her husband were blessed with the birth of Emily. All lived with Cristina's parents in the apartment where she grew up. By that time, her mother and father were older and suffering health problems. Both were diabetics needing insulin. Cristina was their caregiver, a mother, and a full-time tour guide, which took a toll on her marriage.

Meanwhile life in Cuba grew increasingly oppressive, especially for those who, like Cristina's family, opposed the government. Under the U.S. Refugee Program, in 2008 and 2009, four of her siblings and their families emigrated to the States, settling in

Michigan and Florida. However, Cristina, her parents, and her young daughter, Emily, were denied approval.

Around the same time, Cristina decided to divorce her husband. She continued raising Emily, who was only six, while taking care of her parents who were declining rapidly: falling, going blind, and being hospitalized.

After the death of her mother in 2014 and her father in 2018, Cristina's eldest sister, still in Cuba, sold the family's apartment. Thus, Cristina and Emily needed to find another place to live. They stayed with friends for a bit, but then the entire family convinced the older sister to give some of the house sale money to Cristina and Emily to escape. "I had nothing left to lose," she said. "It was time for my daughter and me to leave."

THE JOURNEY: A MOTHER'S SACRIFICE

In 2019, Cristina and her daughter, now seventeen, set out from Cuba, flying to Suriname, which was a safe place for Cubans to come and go. In fact, it was where Cubans could run successful importing and exporting businesses. They both stayed for two years, Cristina working jobs on farms and in kitchens, saving up money from work as well as receiving donations from her family and friends in the United States.

For Cubans to travel to the United States, they must undergo an interview at a U.S. Embassy to obtain a visa. Unfortunately, the U.S. Embassy in Suriname didn't conduct interviews for visas like most other countries. Therefore, the plan of many Cubans was to catch a highly promoted flight from Suriname to Nicaragua to go to the U.S. Embassy there for the interview. The flight tickets were $5,000, but Cristina and Emily knew this was a way to freedom. However, the flight turned out to be an expensive scam. Cristina and Emily lost all that money, but they got to know three other Cubans who were also fooled by the flight. The five of them banded together to embark on the dangerous overland trek through South and Central America.

The overland journey took many months, on every mode of transportation imaginable. The first leg of the trek was by boat from Suriname to Belem, Brazil, in the Amazon. This took seven days. Then, they spent another few weeks traveling by buses, taxis, and planes to Peru, Ecuador, and Colombia. They were always accompanied by "coyotes," who guide immigrants for a price to secretly house them and get them across borders. This beginning of the journey tested them, but it was nothing like the next stage, the Darién Gap.

This seventy-mile section between Colombia and Panama is remote, roadless, and lawless. The Darién Gap is known for steep mountains, deep rainforests, and vast swamps, which are home to venomous snakes, crocodiles, drug cartels, and bandits. However, every year hundreds of thousands of exiles cross it on foot with the help of coyotes. Even though the route is unmarked, the rugged paths through the jungle and across rivers are littered with signs of desperation: lost shoes, abandoned belongings too heavy to carry, and even skulls. It's common to hear of others' stories of death, rape, robberies, and assaults along the route.

One of the most harrowing moments for Cristina and Emily occurred on their first night, climbing La Miel (Honey) Mountain. The perilous route was steep and slippery. Neither Cristina nor Emily was prepared for such a feat nor had adequate footwear. Eventually, Emily stopped and couldn't continue up the steep incline. The combination of the physical stressors and the anxiety of knowing that someone her own age, a seventeen-year-old, had died on the same passage just the day before threw her into panic. "She couldn't breathe; her lips turned purple," Cristina recounted. "I thought she was going to die. I begged her to cry, to let it out. It's the hardest thing, watching your child suffer and feeling powerless." Luckily, the group was patient and helped Cristina calm Emily down. Emily had experienced her first panic attack on that mountain, something neither of them wanted to repeat ever again.

The high-risk journey also brought them face-to-face with death. On the last day in Colombia, one of the coyotes became increasingly frustrated with Cristina's slow pace. By this time, Cristina had ulcers on her feet and had lost all her toenails. This coyote offered to take Cristina on a shortcut, but she felt in her gut that he might secretly take her off and kill her, leaving Emily all alone. Before the coyote separated mother from daughter, Cristina made sure the other three Cubans would watch out for Emily while she took the chance on the shortcut. Every step in pain, Cristina thought of her late mother. "I don't know why, but I told the coyote my mother's story, and how much her death hurt me. Somehow, it changed him. From then on, he stayed by my side and helped me finish the journey."

REACHING THE UNITED STATES: A NEW BEGINNING

After three months of traveling treacherous terrain through eleven countries and experiencing avaricious coyotes, corrupt officials, and scary "safehouses," they crossed the Rio Grande into Texas. They spent days in a detention processing center before flying to Michigan to reunite with family. Though physically and emotionally battered, they were determined to rebuild their lives.

They stayed in Michigan for two months with one sister but knew that Florida would be better in the long term. Making the move to Florida, they stayed with one sister for two more months and then a brother for another two months, before eventually finding a place of their own outside of Tampa.

LIFE IN FLORIDA: REDISCOVERING PURPOSE

In Florida, Cristina works at Walmart, and Emily, a driven and resilient young woman, earned her GED within months of arriving. She's now pursuing higher education and thriving as a cashier in retail. "I always tell her," Cristina said, "you're going to achieve so much more than I ever could. That's why I did this."

Emily proudly admitted, "I have become a strong woman thanks to the journey—all of it."

LESSONS IN RESILIENCE: THE LOOK UP MANTRA

Reflecting on their journey of nearly 7,000 miles, Cristina shared, "Every obstacle has a lesson. When Emily had her panic attack, it taught me to stay calm for her. When the coyote nearly gave up on me, my mother's memory saved me." When asked how she faces challenges now, Cristina says, "Whatever comes now is nothing compared to what I have overcome already. Nothing compares. Nothing."

Emily added, "Remember, no matter how hard life can be, never give up. Make your life worth it. Take advantage of every opportunity. Give the best of you every day."

Their story embodies the *Look Up* mantra because they both believe that amidst the most difficult challenges, there's always a glimmer of light. For Cristina, that light is her daughter's future. "I wanted freedom for her," she declares. "We're building a life where she can look up and dream without limits."

ABOUT CRISTINA AND EMILY RODRIGUEZ

Both Cristina and Emily were born in Santiago de Cuba. Both immigrated to the United States in 2021 and are currently living outside of Tampa, Florida. Cristina is a proud mother, sister, colleague, and friend to many. She is known for her positive attitude, smile, and humor. Emily is embracing her new country and its opportunities for education and employment. She dreams of building off her GED to go to college and have a successful career in finance.

PART 3:

DISCOVERING EXCEPTIONAL STRENGTH

ON YOUR MARK.
GET SET. GO.
CATHERINE FRANCIS

In the fall of 2007, everything seemed to be going swimmingly for Catherine Francis at her suburban high school in Tewksbury, Massachusetts. As a junior, she was one of the top students in her class and had a tight group of girlfriends, a younger sister, two supportive parents, and two cats. She enjoyed the occasional morning run around the neighborhood before school. She considered it a warm-up, as she was an excellent sprinter in the 300 meter run and 50 yard dash on the girls' track team.

Then, at an after-school track practice, life as she knew it stopped. The practice started with a gentle run followed by weight training. Catherine ran strong on the warm-up run but immediately felt fatigued and weak doing weighted lunges.

She just brushed it off and worked through it. Then, she felt a wave of vertigo and breathlessness after exercises on the stairs. Something wasn't right. Her right side was acting funny, both her arm and leg. Plus, she was extremely thirsty. Her workout gear was drenched. She was sweating through her workout clothing but felt cold. Catherine began to see yellow spots. Was she dehydrated? Something was definitely wrong. Two friends noticed, gave her water, and called the coach. Meanwhile Catherine's head pounded, and she was in excruciating pain. The coach called 911 while one of her girlfriends called Catherine's parents. Within minutes, the EMTs arrived, swiftly taking her on a gurney to the ambulance and on to the hospital.

That was the last memory Catherine had until seven days later.

THE KNOWN AND UNKNOWN

When Catherine's parents arrived at the hospital, the doctor explained she had suffered a brain aneurysm. At birth, Catherine had an arteriovenous malformation (AVM), which grew larger in time, causing the aneurysm. The doctor continued informing them of the known—and worse—the unknown. The right side of her body was paralyzed, and she was in an induced coma to reduce brain swelling. If or when she woke up, the doctor explained that Catherine may not be able to communicate, which the doctor called aphasia. "We don't know," he lamented. "She may never wake up."

Family, friends, and coaches stopped by the ICU to show their support, but Catherine was still in a coma. Finally, on day seven, she awoke and was in tremendous shock. "What happened?" she wondered. "How long have I been here?"

Her doctor came in immediately to assess her strength, movement, and eyesight. No movement with the right leg. The same for the right arm. Catherine woke up severely different than she was a week ago, and she wanted answers but couldn't form the questions. She tried to communicate, but either nothing or gibberish would come out. Not only was Catherine paralyzed, but she was also mute. The doctor suggested getting started with speech therapy as soon as possible.

RETURN FROM NOTHINGNESS

After a difficult month in the hospital, Catherine regained her ability to speak, but she still had problems reading, putting clear thoughts together, and recalling words. She had progressed enough, however, to be moved from the ICU to the children's wing to start physical therapy.

For a track runner, a treadmill was nothing to be afraid of, but for the new Catherine it was terrifying. Heather, her physical therapist, had to convince Catherine that this was the only way to regain her mobility. Afraid and thinking she was going to fall, Catherine struggled to get on the treadmill, gripping the guardrail with her left hand. When the treadmill started up, her left leg had a smooth cadence, but her right would land heavily. She didn't go fast, but she did it. Catherine later shared that over the next five months, she "envisioned racing my closest friend on a track and not a treadmill. I'd hear the 'on your mark, get set,' and then the gunshot. Then, I would close my eyes. I was in the moment and in my element. All I could think about was the race, not the treadmill."

With tenacity, positivity, and support from her family, Catherine was able to leave the hospital on New Year's Day, 2008. She continued physical therapy, speech therapy, and tutoring at home until the spring, when she challenged herself to return to school with a half-time schedule. Like a typical teenager, Catherine didn't want the other students to treat her differently because of her cane. Before her first day back, she toured the high school with Heather and her parents. She tested herself and proved to them she could return to school without her cane.

PERSISTENCE, POSITIVITY, AND PURPOSE

Fast forward to her senior year of high school, and Catherine was taking a full load of classes. She was accepted to attend the Rochester Institute of Technology. At her high school graduation, Catherine was awarded art student of the year, with a standing ovation for her extraordinary physical, mental, and emotional achievements.

When asked about the perspective gained from her teenage health scare and her connection to *Look Up,* she explained, "When you're paralyzed on the right side of your body, it's very easy to be pessimistic, to feel lost, and to give up. *Believing* is one of the most powerful things. Putting a smile on—despite how crummy I felt—made everyone feel better, and in turn, made *me* feel better." Catherine's life-changing experience inspired her to write her first book, *The Day I Died.*

Catherine still encounters challenges because of her AVM. She wears a brace to walk, which everyone can see. However, it's her invisible mental disability that poses roadblocks for her, especially with people she doesn't know. She added, "I often need to ask for people to repeat what they said, especially with questions. Some people are patient. Others not so much." When asked about life lessons from her aneurysm, Catherine said, "It was a catalyst to many positive things. I survived this, so I'm here for a reason. One of the many reasons is to teach in the classroom, but another is to share my stories through my books."

ABOUT CATHERINE FRANCIS

Catherine Francis was born and raised in the suburbs of Boston. She graduated from Rochester Institute of Technology with her BFA in film and animation as well as an MEd in Elementary Education. Currently, she is an English language arts elementary teacher in Massachusetts. Loving the power of words, Catherine has also authored three books: *The Day I Died, One Term Left,* and *The Night at Times Square.* Find out more about Catherine and her books on Amazon under C.M. Francis.

THERE'S NOTHING SO BAD BUT WHAT THERE'S SOME GOOD IN IT

LESLEY, LORNA, AND LINDA

Lesley and Steve Hackett had a busy suburban Twin Cities household with two children, Kaitlin, eight, and David, six. Lesley balanced being a mom with community activities and Bible study, while Steve had a successful career in medical research and development. With the kids going back to school in the fall of 2003, Lesley was going to return to her Human Resources career. She was thirty-five.

LESLEY

That October, the Hackett's were home when Lesley's oncology doctor called. He explained Lesley's recent lab results, which had revealed many lumps, some of which were highly invasive. He diagnosed Lesley as having aggressive breast cancer, which had spread to her lymph nodes. This meant a 15 percent chance of living five years unless treated immediately.

"My body was in shock from the news," said Lesley. "My hands trembled for a few days. I wasn't able to sleep. Steve was unable to work while trying to process everything," Lesley shared about that unforgettable day. It was also Breast Cancer Awareness month, and Lesley and her family were bombarded with reminders of the grave statistics. This made it even more emotionally painful while enduring the whirlwind of doctor appointments, MRIs, CAT scans, X-rays, surgeries, and blood tests.

BREAST CANCER, A LONG ROAD TO HEALING

Over the next three years, Lesley underwent chemotherapy, radiation, a double mastectomy, and reconstructive surgery, followed by five years of Tamoxifen (hormone) therapy. "I wanted it all to be over as soon as possible," she recounted, "but various treatments kept dragging out the process. I lost track of surgeries after fourteen procedures."

To lend a helping hand, many people offered prayers from near and as far away as Cambodia. To remind herself of all this powerful support, Lesley made a paper prayer chain with each person's name on it. Before each of her surgeries, Lesley reflected on her thankfulness for all God's blessings: her kids, husband, family, and friends.

As a side effect of the chemotherapy, Lesley lost her hair. She would wear a wig and pencil in her eyebrows so she wouldn't scare the children, particularly her youngest. The wig provided a bit of normalcy—and some humor as well. One evening, while Steve and Lesley lay in their bed, Steve said, "I feel like I'm cheating on my wife!" They both burst out laughing. From that evening on, the wig was known as "Trixie." Such spontaneity goes to show that being in the moment and laughing is the best medicine.

During this period, the Hacketts received an outpouring of help: Friends from church brought dinners over a few times a week. Coworkers at Steve's job collected money the Hacketts used for a maid service. Steve's parents helped by babysitting the kids during surgeries and driving the kids to school as well as Lesley to some appointments. Lesley's mom, Lorna Treptow, who had also suffered breast cancer, helped around the house with chores, babysitting, and meals.

LORNA

At forty-two, Lorna was living with her husband Richard and her son Brian in Indianapolis when she was diagnosed with breast cancer. In fact, her family had a history of breast cancer.

Lorna's mother had breast cancer at forty-eight, and her paternal grandmother had breast cancer at ninety before that. Lorna explained, "I was only fifteen when *my* mother suddenly passed away from metastatic cancer after only four months of illness. It was a shock to both my father and me." Although it was a trying time for both Lorna and her father, she remembered her wise mother saying, "There's nothing so bad but what there's some good in it." The upside, or the good, in this case was that Lorna and her father became closer; plus, she knew her risks and proactively got checked.

Then, in the spring of 1989, with both of her daughters, Lesley and Linda, in college and her youngest son Brian, fourteen, Lorna herself was diagnosed with breast cancer. Because of her early diagnosis and a physician who instilled confidence in her, she underwent surgery to remove the cancer. Afterward, she received thirty-eight radiation treatments.

On the day of the surgery, Richard called her. He announced, "You are the winner of a one-hundred-dollar prize in the local radio station's contest." Lorna took that as a good omen that everything would be okay. She didn't fear for her life. She trusted God. Fortunately, with no spreading of cancer into her lymph nodes, Lorna was deemed cancer free after one surgery and radiation treatments.

LINDA

Having known of her mother's cancer when going off to college and her sister Lesley's cancer in her mid-thirties, Linda Biery was fearful of a similar diagnosis. However, she didn't let it get in the way of raising a family of four. Nor did she let it stop her from writing music and leading a Christian summer camp in Pennsylvania called Summer's Best 2 Weeks.

In 2010, when she was thirty-nine, Linda was also diagnosed with breast cancer. When Linda found out, her knees immediately went limp. She called her husband Kent and had him come home immediately. They both sat on their porch swing and cried. Later, they told their kids about the cancer. Kendra, the oldest child and only daughter, was scared. "It was Kendra's biggest fear that I would get cancer," said Linda. However, the boys—Jonathan, Joshua, and CJ—were oblivious, probably because of their young age.

Having Lesley, Lorna, and Kent as support, Linda navigated her way through various doctors and clinics to find the right treatment. In Linda's case, she opted to have a double mastectomy and reconstructive surgery like her sister. However, her two-and-a-half-year journey was not without its unexpected trials. The first surgeon failed to remove all the golf-ball-sized masses, so Linda needed additional surgery to completely get rid of the cancerous tumors. In fact, this same doctor made four critical mistakes, prompting Linda to seek another doctor in Pittsburgh. During this time, Linda turned to God, prayer chains, running, and music to find the upside. As a songwriter, she wrote the song "Big Enough," which follows Linda and her family through diagnosis, surgery, and recovery. Its chorus reflects how she faced these trying times:

God you are . . .
Big enough
For the toughest times
And strong enough
For the pain
And bright enough
To be our sunshine
Through the rain.

Once Linda was cancer free, she felt truly blessed. She considered it a gift and an invitation to live life and live it large. She went snowboarding, ripsticking (similar to skateboarding), and other adventures that reinforced the beauty of having a second chance at life. She didn't mind that some led to bumps, bruises, concussions, and other injuries. Linda shared, "Looking back at my life, I have no regrets."

THE LOOK UP MANTRA

Older sister Lesley explained the connection to the *Look Up* mantra: "Even in a difficult situation, if you focus on all the blessings God has given you instead of the challenges you're going through, you feel grateful instead of having an attitude of poor me or why me. You appreciate the beauty or brighter side of things, the positives, the light in the darkness, the upside."

As Lorna's mother said, "There's nothing so bad but what there's some good in it." To help their daughters and, in turn, other women, Lorna, Lesley, and Linda have done genetic testing. All remain cancer free. Although they can never remove all worry, the upside is for the next generation: Lesley's daughter Kaitlin and Linda's daughter Kendra have access to more information, better treatment, frequent checkups, and the sage advice of not one but three brave family members.

ABOUT LORNA, LESLEY, AND LINDA

Lorna Treptow resides in Brooklyn Park, Minnesota, and is a great grandmother of two, grandmother of six, and mother of three. She's enjoying her retirement, spending time with family and friends.

Also in Minnesota, one of Lorna's daughters, Lesley Hackett, has been happily married to Steve for thirty-three years as of this writing. They have two adult children in their twenties and two grandchildren, and Lesley has a cream golden retriever, Chloe, a trained therapy dog. Professionally, Lesley is an executive recruiter and has worked in talent acquisition for over fifteen years.

Lesley's sister, Linda Biery, lives in rural Pennsylvania with her husband Kent, and they're proud of their four children. Both dedicate most of their time to the Christian sports camp Summer's Best 2 Weeks. You can find Linda's music on Spotify.

GOT TO
MOVE FORWARD
DR. DEREK RIEBAU

On the outskirts of Nashville, Tennessee, Derek Riebau has a full plate. He's a busy family man with a challenging career as the medical director of the Stroke Center at prestigious Vanderbilt University Medical Center. He and his wife Sarah are raising three girls, currently sixteen, fifteen, and eleven. Derek works in his neurological specialty, caring for patients in the hospital one week each month.

While at the medical center, Derek takes on additional responsibilities of not only training residents and medical school students but doing administrative work. On the other weeks, Derek works from home as an on-call telestroke specialist, using videoconferencing to care for patients at hospitals throughout the country. His in-person rounds at the medical center are especially demanding as he's on call twenty-four hours a day. He's routinely awakened in the middle of the night to review brain scans and guide the next steps for emergency management of patients who have symptoms of a stroke. Every second counts when dealing with a stroke. However, his road to becoming a successful physician, husband, and father was surely not without serious roadblocks.

HOW IT ALL BEGAN

Rewind to the early '90s. In his early years at the University of Wisconsin at Eau Claire in western Wisconsin, Derek wasn't very concerned about grades. Playing soccer, skiing, and partying with friends took precedence over studying. His grades were better than passing but certainly not worth celebrating. In the fall of his sophomore year, Derek noticed a numbing sensation in his right hand, and his writing became sloppy. Initially, he brushed off the unusual symptoms. By the winter break, the numbness had expanded up his arm to his face. This led to an appointment with a neurologist, who ordered an MRI of the brain and spinal cord, which revealed a possible tumor in his spinal cord. The next step was to meet with a neurosurgeon. Before that appointment, Derek enjoyed a ski trip to Colorado with friends. It didn't cross his mind that it would be his last time skiing.

When Derek returned home, the neurosurgeon advised surgery for the suspected spinal cord tumor. "I wasn't too concerned," recalls Derek. "I just wanted to get through surgery, recover, and get back to campus."

A LIFE-CHANGING EVENT

On February 4, 1993, Derek underwent surgery, and his nineteen-year-old life changed forever. He awoke from anesthesia paralyzed. He couldn't move his legs and had minimal movement in his arms. In the process of resecting the spinal cord tumor, swelling and pressure on the spinal cord had caused a C-6/7 spinal cord injury.

During the first couple of days, Derek was groggy from a combination of steroids and pain medications. Over the next few months in the hospital, he came to the realization of life with a devastating spinal cord injury, although he was not facing this challenge alone. In addition to family visiting daily, numerous friends from college made the short journey from the dorms to the hospital a few hundred yards away, rotating each night of the week for two to three months, to provide a constant vigil of support. Then followed many months of in-patient rehabilitation, including admission to Shephard Center, a specialized rehabilitation facility for spinal injuries in Atlanta. Although Derek progressed to being able to stand up from his wheelchair with support, he would not walk again.

Derek left Atlanta to return to a new life in a familiar place. The first step was living with his parents in Wisconsin to learn how to do normal things in a different way. After a year with his parents, he got an apartment close to campus and resumed college. While Derek was on his own, his parents were still close; plus, he had many friends who stopped by regularly and assisted him on campus. During this rehabilitation and transition phase, Derek wasn't depressed or angry but rather realistic about this new life. "No option but to move forward," he said. In Atlanta, Derek had met a wise man, also in a wheelchair, who introduced the term "comparative reality." This man advised: "At this point, you're constantly comparing how you are now to how you were then. It may take years, but over time that will evolve, whereby you'll no longer compare your disabled self to your pre-disabled self and life will be more normal."

A NEW PASSION IS BORN

Before his surgery, Derek had thought about becoming a psychologist. However, after his experience in the healthcare system, as devastating as that was personally, he acquired a passion and drive to care for those in similar circumstances. "Maybe the upside is that, had this not happened, I may not have had the mindset to study, focus, and accomplish what's needed to even get into medical school."

Derek graduated from Eau Claire and landed a highly sought-after spot in the University of Wisconsin School of Medicine. Upon graduation in 2002, after four years of medical school (and many years of snow and cold in Wisconsin), Derek moved to Nashville, Tennessee, for the next stage of training. He secured a residency in the Department of Neurology at Vanderbilt University Medical Center.

The move to Music City was not only a great move professionally but romantically. During his second year of residency, he met his now wife. Sarah and Derek first met while eating dinner with friends at a downtown Nashville restaurant and immediately hit it off. Just over a year later, they married.

LIFE KEEPS LOOKING UP

In the same month as their wedding, Derek completed his residency and remained on staff as an assistant professor of neurology at Vanderbilt University Medical Center. In another two years, Derek and Sarah started a family with the birth of the first of their three girls.

In explaining his connection to *Look Up,* Derek shared, "My reality is what it is. I wasn't then and to this day am not going to let my spinal cord injury get me down." He admitted that medical school and residency were tough, but not as tough as the initial months and years after he awoke from surgery paralyzed. He established a new normal and was able to tap into a keen focus and steadfast drive, with no looking back, only looking forward. Derek hopes his story will inspire his three girls and the readers of this book. "You can't let things stand in your way," he advises. "If you encounter an obstacle, find a way around it and keep moving forward. If I can do it, you can, too."

ABOUT DR. DEREK RIEBAU

Dr. Derek Riebau is an associate professor of neurology and medical director of the Stroke Center at Vanderbilt University Medical Center. In addition to his clinical duties, Dr. Riebau has been heavily involved in education at Vanderbilt University School of Medicine and the Vanderbilt University School of Nursing. He has received numerous awards and honors for his teaching. He was twice the recipient of the Shovel Award, given by the graduating medical school class to the faculty member they identify as having the most positive and meaningful influence on their education. At home, Derek and his wife Sarah are proud parents of three beautiful young ladies.

FINDING THE GIFT
IN MY SITUATION

MICHELLE MANN

In 2015, Michelle Mann was driving her trusty 2002 Dodge Ram 1500 truck on a rural desert road in southern Arizona with her four-year-old son in the back seat. It was starting to get dark when she noticed a vehicle in front of her try to run over an endangered lizard called a gila monster (pronounced hee-lah monster), and it was injured. Many people don't like gila monsters because their bite is poisonous, but Michelle stopped to help it get to safety. She stepped out of the car to evaluate how she could get the lizard off the road without endangering herself. While she was formulating a plan, a man and woman arrived at the scene. Both the couple and Michelle agreed that the lizard needed to be moved so no other drivers could harm it.

The couple noticed the small boy in the back seat of Michelle's truck and offered to take care of moving the lizard so she could get him home for bedtime. That was just the first encounter with these good Samaritans.

In 2017, Michelle was once again driving home on a dark night after watching a movie with her husband. They had driven separate vehicles, which wasn't uncommon as their relationship was growing more and more distant despite counseling. Michelle was on her way to pick up her son when she heard a divine voice say, "Michelle, you're going to get hit, but everything is going to be okay." Now nervous, she continued driving and then saw the headlights of three cars coming toward her vehicle. The first car passed her in the opposing lane, but the second car swerved into her truck. For a brief second, Michelle had a vision of the driver—his face, hair, and even his pain. Then, she blacked out.

Luckily, the third car's driver called 911, because the driver of the second car needed to be airlifted out to a trauma hospital. An ambulance came and took Michelle to the hospital, where she found out she had a fractured C6 vertebra and a brain injury that impacted her vision.

VANISHING DREAMS TURN TO SPIRITUAL INSPIRATION

In time, Michelle discovered the crash had taken place at a collective speed of 100 miles per hour, and the other driver was a local drunk prone to such behavior. She counted her blessings, but that was just the beginning of her troubles.

The car accident triggered a ripple effect of change and loss. Michelle's husband walked out, leaving her to care for a mortgaged house and a young boy with special needs. She was disabled and could no longer work as a real estate agent as she had before. "My dreams I had hoped for up until then vanished," she said.

For about seven years, Michelle was homebound. She relied on others to help with getting her son to and from special events and driving her to doctor appointments. She had an empty garage as she didn't have a car nor the money to buy one. It was during this quarantine that Michelle learned to surrender, accept help, and reconnect to the universe and her spiritual nature.

For inspiration, she tapped into her previous decades of working with Native Americans. She had helped the grandmothers prepare hot stones for their sweat lodges. She now rekindled this connection to the Native American teachings and commitment to cherishing Mother Nature. In fact, shortly after her accident, Michelle had been taken under the wing of a Sundance Lakota Dakota medicine man and chief with thirty-plus years of experience. He helped Michelle heal all aspects of herself through the native teachings.

One day, while looking out into the desert from her home, she heard the same voice she'd heard the night of the accident, saying, "Grow where I planted you." Michelle jokingly replied, "Sure. Grow in the desert where nothing grows." However, because her life had stopped and gone quiet, she focused on what the gift was in this part of her life.

DOWN BUT NOT OUT

By 2019, Michelle and her son were down to their last $400 and barely had milk in the refrigerator. Someone told her about the Food Bank, and she contacted them. When she met two women during the Food Bank evaluation, one offered to take care of her son's flat bicycle tire, arranging to come by with her husband.

A couple of weeks later, Michelle and the wife chatted inside while the husband fixed the flat tire in the garage. When he finished, the man came in and asked Michelle, "Were you the woman who was driving the big black truck and saw the injured gila monster?" Shocked, Michelle said, "Yes . . . but how did you know that?"

"We're the couple that stopped to help you," he replied, much to her surprise.

Over time, their friendship expanded, and the man suggested Michelle may want to paint her garage floor because someone might have a use for it and want to rent it from her.

Well, she did paint it, and a seed was planted. She just wasn't aware of what it would produce yet.

SACRED CIRCLES

Not too long after painting her garage floor, Michelle shared her instructions, "Grow where I planted you," with her medicine man friend. He suggested she open up her garage for Sacred Circles. Reluctantly, Michelle agreed to hold the circles for four months on a donations basis and see what presented itself. After the seventh Sacred Circle, Michelle's native guide offered her the opportunity to run the circles with his sacred medicine altar and the sacred medicine wheel. This wheel bridges heaven and Earth within oneself using the five-pointed star and the virtues that embody those directions.

What started out as an empty garage became a beautiful temple where, at the time of this writing, Michelle has hosted over two dozen monthly Sacred Circles, helping others connect to themselves at their core. Michelle shared, "The universe is always giving us signs. The accident brought me back to the present. Because my life had stopped and gone quiet, I focused on what gift my life had to offer me."

Her connection to *Look Up?* "My whole life has been about finding the gift in my situation."

ABOUT MICHELLE MANN

Michelle is a healer and practitioner of Native American and non-traditional healing techniques. She lives in Vail, Arizona, where she hosts monthly healing circles called Sacred Circles. Also, Michelle is the proud mother of a teenage boy. Together they love to enjoy nature. From overcoming her perception of darkness from a traumatic accident and much heartbreak, she teaches others to remember that there is light. This message inspires us all to remember who we are and where we came from. The Truth is within us. Connect with Michelle Mann and her Sacred Circles on Facebook.

FALL DOWN SEVEN TIMES, STAND UP EIGHT

P.J.

In 2013 in Noda, Japan, at the Bujinkan International Hombu Dojo, P.J. and Rob, both 10th-degree Black Belts, were asked to take the floor and demonstrate a technique. In front of their sensei, 150 spectators, and a film crew, Rob punched P.J., and a moment later he found himself on the floor of the dojo.

Their sensei wanted everyone to understand the power of the human spirit, so he grabbed a wooden sword and handed it to Rob. Understanding his sensei's intent—and without the traditional bow to initiate a match—Rob immediately spun around with a full speed surprise attack and attempted to cut P.J.'s head off. The attack was so fast and unexpected by everyone in the dojo that P.J. recalls hearing an audible gasp from the crowd. Instinctively, he tucked his head and dropped below the blade. In that same instant, P.J. turned to face the oncoming attack so the sword wouldn't clip the back of his skull as it passed overhead. P.J. heard the wooden sword cut through the air just above him and felt the side of the blade as it faintly tickled the surface of his left ear. With lightning-fast reflexes, P.J. trapped Rob's wrist between his chin and right shoulder before a second sword cut could come. He then skillfully separated his attacker from his weapon and brought Rob to the floor again. P.J. had again turned the tables on his surprised opponent!

A grand applause ensued for the winner, P.J., forty-four, who had studied martial arts since his first year of college. He had dreamed of being a ninja since he was ten years old, but his father said he couldn't because he was "handicapped" and, at the time, walked with leg braces. Many don't know the word "ninja" means "person who perseveres"—in essence, a person who doesn't quit—and P.J. is a real-life ninja.

NOT TAKING DISABILITY FOR AN ANSWER

As a young child, P.J. was diagnosed with a rare form of muscular dystrophy (MD). The doctors predicted he wouldn't live past the age of seven. Instead of losing his life, however, he persevered. He went to school with leg braces, challenging what doctors had advised his parents. During these formative years, it was his mother and her unwavering and encouraging love that forced P.J. to be independent. He got dressed by himself, and eventually he threw those leg braces into the trash can. From early in his childhood, P.J. began speaking on stage and television, encouraging others to live their life bigger and bolder than they had been up to that point.

Sadly, however, by the time P.J. was twelve, he had been in and out of hospitals seventeen times. Every time he became ill, he never fully recovered. Each time, he lost a little bit of mobility and/or strength, which forced him to accept a "new normal." By eighth grade, he needed an electric wheelchair, which he initially hated and called the "electric chair," meaning his prison. However, it provided P.J. with the freedom to move about more easily, graduate high school, and go to college. There, he promptly exchanged his "electric chair" for a manual wheelchair and immediately became a wheelchair athlete in various sports, including martial arts.

THE MAGIC OF MARTIAL ARTS

The martial arts have been extremely instrumental in P.J.'s life. In fact, he has traveled to Japan over a dozen times to train with a real-life ninja master. When asked about that 2013 demonstration, P.J. shared, "I was focused and fully present. There is power in being present." Undoubtedly, technique was also in play during the exchange. "I got Rob to a weak spot and capitalized on his vulnerability," said P.J. However, the martial arts involve far more than techniques and self-defense. When asked about his connection to the martial arts, P.J. quoted the Japanese proverb, "Nana korobi, ya oki," or "Fall down seven times, stand up eight." At its essence, the martial arts represent the philosophy of not quitting, choosing not to give up hope, and always striving for more. Martial arts and other Japanese arts train practitioners to be calm and present as a way of mastering the art and oneself.

Throughout P.J.'s life, he has experienced several pivotal *Look Up* moments in which he implemented being present and finding the upside. The first was in 1998 in Tucson, when he was hit by an SUV, ejected from his wheelchair, and tossed into three lanes of oncoming traffic. As he flew through the air, he could hear his wheelchair behind him crumpling underneath the front of the vehicle. The SUV's front wheel came to rest leaning against his pelvis bone. Had the SUV rolled two more inches, it would've crushed P.J.'s pelvis and lower spine. Fortunately, an EMT team saw the event happen, came rushing to his aid, and took him across the street to a hospital ER.

The next four months tested P.J.'s confidence and drive. He had been teaching people to live at a higher level through his motivational speaking, but in those months of physical therapy, he struggled to keep his mind in the moment and find the upside because he was in so much pain. The very last day of physical therapy, the therapist was able to identify the problem.

When P.J. hit the concrete with the driver's wheel atop him, his hip had popped out of joint. As soon as the therapist popped his hip back into place, all the pain immediately went away. He was ecstatic: "I was filled with an overwhelming sense of gratitude and real love for myself and my life again! This event gave me the opportunity to genuinely appreciate, not take for granted, what I have—even if it may be limited by my disability."

ANOTHER SERIOUS SETBACK

Life seemed back to his new normal until P.J. awoke one morning in December of 2000.

He had lost the use of his shoulders and hands overnight! He knew his muscular dystrophy was progressive. He understood there would be losses and a decline in his strength as he aged, but this was a rude awakening. Just the day before, he had been able to hold a bar of soap in either hand with arms fully extended to shoulder height.

That morning, P.J. had no hand nor shoulder strength. It was erased just like that. Nothing, nada, zilch. In that moment, living alone, he had to find a way to live his life with this new loss. At first, he thought his life was rapidly coming to an end, and he wasn't accepting this easily. He had learned to love his life and wasn't ready to lose it.

Over the next three months, he learned to write with his mouth, push his wheelchair differently, get dressed and undressed differently, and climb in and out of the shower and onto the toilet differently. After he got past the fear, sadness, and worry, P.J. explained, "I was able to reembrace the possibilities and see the upside again! I was still very much alive!"

P.J. embraced this next new normal with even *more* curiosity and zest for life. Despite his disability, he made sure to live well, which meant living in the now, or as he expressed it, "live like your hair is on fire." Thus, P.J. has continued to travel, gone outdoor and indoor skydiving, aqua jetpacking, and the adventure list goes on and on. He was even nominated to carry the Olympic Torch through Tucson in 2002.

YET ANOTHER NEW CHALLENGE TO CONQUER

Then, a trip to Las Vegas, Nevada, in March of 2019 turned his world upside down—again. He caught an unknown virus and within a matter of weeks had lost 85 percent of his physical strength and 50 percent of his lung capacity. Once again, P.J. thought he might not live through it. He lost the ability to roll over in bed. He could no longer get himself up from the ground. Nor could he get in and out of the shower by himself. He could no longer even sit back in his wheelchair and hold himself up without help. Previously, P.J. had needed an hour of personal care in the mornings, but with this recent decline, he needed twenty-four-hour care. With this loss of independence, P.J. started waking up in the middle of the night riddled with anxiety and panic. Something new. He had never experienced panic attacks before. P.J. leveraged his background in meditation and mindfulness to overcome these moments. He shared, "To shift out of the anxiety, fear, and worry, I brought myself back to the moment. We all have a choice about how we feel, no matter our current situation."

Although P.J. has not regained much of his strength or lung capacity, he once again has learned to adapt to another new normal. Thankfully, he no longer experiences anxiety or panic attacks. Also, he has whittled his personal care hours down to approximately two per day. "To roll over in your bed, sit up, and put your feet on the floor beside your bed in the morning is a great way to start your day," said P.J. "I struggle every single day just to sit up. It takes me ten minutes," he added.

If P.J. works that hard to sit up to start every day, maybe the difficulties or challenges *we* are facing can be overcome by being in the moment and living with gratitude. As P.J. states, "Change is inevitable. Transformation is a choice."

ABOUT P.J.

P.J. is an international speaker and success strategist—who focuses on results! Despite his disability, he truly lives an extraordinary life: sailing, outdoor skydiving, indoor skydiving, trapezing, ziplining, hiking, mountain climbing, snow skiing, water skiing, aqua jetpacking, and the list goes on! He's a former wheelchair athlete, an international traveler, an amateur watercolorist, and the founder of two nonprofit organizations and four sports programs for the disabled. He's also a published author, 10th-degree Black Belt, martial arts and women's self-defense instructor, and meditation teacher. Additionally, P.J. is now training law enforcement officers. He created a completely unique course that teaches officers how to successfully interact with physically disabled suspects. Nowhere else in the world does this training exist! To learn more about P.J.'s speaking, coaching, and law enforcement training, visit *www.pjswisdom.com.*

LESSONS FROM A SURVIVOR

MARIAH FORSTER OLSON

In 1987, eight-year-old Mariah was in second grade, living in a small Midwestern town. She lost her first tooth, started piano lessons, and was loved by her two parents and younger brother Gabriel. This childhood life seems normal, but Mariah was far from an average second grader, because that year, she was pronounced cancer free.

In 1980, Mariah and her parents discovered that a large tumor had been growing out of Mariah's spine. The tumor wrapped around a portion of her heart, and pushed against her windpipe and lungs, making it difficult to breathe. Eventually, after several misdiagnoses at a local medical facility, an X-ray finally revealed the problem, and Mariah's parents were advised to immediately take her to the Mayo Clinic in Rochester, Minnesota. There, she was diagnosed with neuroblastoma, a type of childhood cancer that consists of a solid tumor. It's the most common type of cancer in infants, but neuroblastoma is often deadly. Although children are often born with it, they typically don't know they have it until the cancer is more advanced and has grown and metastasized to other areas of the body.

On the day Mariah was diagnosed, doctors at Mayo Clinic acted immediately, intending to remove the tumor with surgery. However, they found the tumor was so large and intricately wrapped around many key, vital areas, that the surgery couldn't proceed. Instead, Mariah's medical team opted to try to shrink the tumor with multiple rounds of radiation before attempting a second surgery to remove it, about two months after the initial attempt.

CHALLENGING ODDS AGAINST SURVIVAL

Despite the removal of the majority of her tumor and additional rounds of radiation, the medical team informed Mariah's parents that her odds of survival were still low and additional treatments were needed. Very limited treatment options were available in the early '80s, but the doctors presented a way to raise Mariah's odds of survival. They offered a clinical trial, which consisted of two years of a new chemotherapy protocol. At that time, it was simply called an "experimental treatment."

Mariah shares, "Chemotherapy was the only part of my cancer that I remember because the nausea was so intense and brutal.

I would carry around an empty, one-gallon ice cream bucket as my "puke pail." Mariah's third birthday coincided with her last chemotherapy visit at her local treatment facility. Her doctor and nurse purchased a cake, and Mariah thought they were simply celebrating her birthday rather than also celebrating the momentous occasion of finishing two years of cancer treatments! Today, many people ring a bell when they finish their cancer treatments, but Mariah exclaimed, "Instead, I got a cake, presents, and a private birthday party with my doctor, nurse, and other medical professionals!"

For the next five years, Mariah was under close monitoring and regularly scheduled testing. Neuroblastoma has a high relapse rate, and it was difficult to predict what could happen given Mariah's treatments, especially the experimental chemotherapy trial. Fortunately, without a recurrence or relapse for five years from her last treatment, Mariah was deemed cancer free at the age of eight. "I am so appreciative and blessed that I survived," she said. "My Mayo doctor told me I was one of the few lucky ones. That said, it's important to note that although childhood cancer occurs during childhood, the effects of it last a lifetime."

FIFTY-TWO SURGERIES

At the time of this writing, Mariah was in her mid-forties. She had had fifty-two surgeries and around one hundred different medical conditions, and most of them are related to her cancer and its treatments. She endures severe, chronic, excruciating nerve, muscle, and bone pain. Mariah needs to use a cane for short distances and/or a wheelchair for longer distances. The pain is present every minute out of every hour, and every hour of every day, so she can never escape it.

Yet, Mariah's experiences and medical issues aren't unique. Most childhood cancer survivors experience at least one or more serious medical conditions from their treatments. Ramifications from childhood cancer treatments can be horrific. In addition to physical effects, many deal with anxiety, depression, and other psychosocial effects.

MUSIC TO THE RESCUE

In childhood, Mariah dove into music to find joy. In middle school, she added the oboe to her piano playing. Although she occasionally still plays the piano, she continues to regularly play the oboe. This has opened her world to playing in several area ensembles and meeting new friends, which is how Mariah met her husband Troy. For their wedding, Mariah's oboe teacher, a Julliard graduate, skillfully and beautifully played "Gabriel's Oboe" as the bride walked down the aisle.

No doubt, one of Mariah's loves and sources of meditation is music. "It allows me to focus and get my emotions out," she says. Similarly, with regard to the *Look Up* mantra, Mariah asserts, "Life is all about perspective. Norman Vincent Peale, an American optimist and minister, said, 'Change your thoughts and you change your world.' I could dwell on the difficult parts of my life; I certainly battle them every day. Yet, I would rather focus on hope, optimism, and positivity. Music is one way that I am able to that!"

Professionally, Mariah works with several nonprofits to conquer neuroblastoma and childhood cancer in general, as well as fight for childhood cancer survivors. Her ultimate goal is to help patients, survivors, and families feel less alone and isolated, because that has been her family's battle. "I want to make it just a little easier for the childhood cancer community, compared to what my family and I experienced," Mariah explains.

SHARING TO HELP OTHERS

Mariah was diagnosed with cancer when there was little hope for survival. She explains, "I feel as if I survived for a reason. Now, my nonprofit work with childhood cancer keeps me busy, and it also gives me a sense of purpose. It fills my heart to fight for past, present, and future childhood cancer patients and survivors, as well as their families, and I feel as if this is what I have been called to do with my life."

When asked what advice Mariah would give others going through a similar trying situation, she breaks it down into four parts:

- "Feel the full spectrum of emotions, from the cries to the laughs, but ultimately strive to focus on hope, optimism, and positivity.
- Find your inner circle, whether friends, family, pets, or others.
- Find a hobby or something that can help you navigate the difficulties in life the way music does for me.

- Take the focus off yourself by helping others."

In September 2022, Mariah signed a publishing contract to share her story in a memoir titled, *Hope Over Despair: Childhood Cancer and the Lifelong Journey of Survivorship.* The book includes more details about her diagnosis, treatments, late effects, and medical conditions, and how they have affected her perspectives on life. In her memoir, Mariah shares how she got through the difficult times then and now in hopes of inspiring others to keep trying and overcome obstacles of all kinds.

ABOUT MARIAH FORSTER OLSON

Mariah Forster Olson lives in Wisconsin with her husband Troy and their Siamese cat Isaac. Her neuroblastoma diagnosis in 1980 as well as the treatments needed to eradicate the cancer from her body, left Mariah with a number of serious medical conditions. Mariah now works with multiple childhood cancer nonprofits to increase awareness, support, advocacy, research, and funding for childhood cancer patients, survivors, and their families. She still plays the oboe, and she recently finished writing her autobiography, *Hope Over Despair: Childhood Cancer and the Lifelong Journey of Survivorship,* with Bell Asteri Publishing. Learn more about Mariah and her book at *www.hopeoverdespair.com.*

LOOK UP
AND AROUND
RHONDA MCGOWAN

In 2018, living in a village called West Salem outside of La Crosse, Wisconsin, Rhonda McGowan was happily married to her husband John. She was also the mother of two boys—Keegan, who was twenty years old and in the Navy, and Shea, a senior in high school. For nearly thirty years, Rhonda had been a Spanish teacher. At the time, she was teaching Spanish at Logan High School in La Crosse and was also the World Language chair, which involved managing a department that taught four languages. In addition, she was global coordinator for study abroad trips. Although her life was busy, Rhonda always made time to run. All her life she had been very athletic and had passed that on to her two sons. It was her way to recharge her battery.

On these daily runs, Rhonda began to notice she felt breathless and was losing stamina. Previously, she'd been able to do these runs with ease, but now she needed to stop and catch her breath. Sometimes, she would even vomit. Thinking *this too shall pass*, Rhonda continued her routine, but even at work she began to feel fatigued and run down. Like many teachers, Rhonda's job wasn't done at the sound of the school bell. Her responsibilities as chair meant attending many meetings after school, extra duties, and working several hours at home each evening and on weekends correcting papers and planning. Her fatigue was not only physical but emotional. She felt underappreciated at work. It seemed as if sometimes students and parents would care but sometimes not. "I was just slogging along," Rhonda recounts.

At the same time, she began to experience swelling in her legs and groin as well as purple spots around her eyes. During this time, the high school librarian insisted Rhonda visit a doctor, specifically a cardiologist.

Shortly thereafter, during a visit from her elder son Keegan, they both went for a run around the neighborhood. He noticed her slower pace, difficulty in breathing, and needing to stop. "What's wrong, Mom?" asked Keegan. "You used to kick butt. You need to get things checked out!" This caused her to see a doctor.

SEARCHING FOR A DIAGNOSIS

At her local hospital, a top cardiologist told Rhonda to go home, that nothing was wrong with her. A cardiologist PA said she had gout. Her internal medicine doctor did a series of

Tier 1-3 blood tests, and the Tier 3 test revealed abnormally high protein numbers. The doctor recommended Rhonda see a rheumatologist.

At this point, it had been approximately a year and a half of visiting numerous doctors and receiving the same diagnosis, or rather misdiagnosis. Rhonda knew something obviously wasn't right.

The morning of her rheumatology appointment, Rhonda had difficulty getting her pants on. Her stomach and groin area were extremely swollen. John drove Rhonda to the La Crosse clinic, both of them desperate to find out what was wrong. Ironically, the attending doctor was a female resident who happened to be married to one of the biology teachers at Rhonda's high school. Rhonda gave her a list of symptoms and tried to hold back her tears but just couldn't. "You have to help me," she cried.

The doctor left the exam room, needing to do some research. She was gone for over an hour, which seemed like an eternity. When she returned, the doctor explained why Rhonda's proteins were so high. However, to make sure, Rhonda would need to go to an oncologist to confirm. At the same clinic, the Oncology Department confirmed by a bone marrow biopsy that she had AL amyloidosis, which is a rare blood disorder. Instead of proteins dissolving, they form fibrils that collect in organs, making them stiff and nonfunctional. No wonder she was breathless: She had congestive heart failure. No wonder her stomach was distended: The doctors confirmed that her colon was not working at all and was backed up. Therefore, an emergency colostomy was performed, allowing her colon to drain. She was also diagnosed with terminal stage-4 cancer, with only nine months to two years to live.

John was speechless. On the other hand, Rhonda was angry. "I've taken care of myself. I run. I eat well. This isn't fair!" On the drive home, they agreed to immediately tell both sons. When Rhonda shared the diagnosis with Shea, he immediately looked down at the ground and went upstairs to his bedroom, not saying a word. She knew the news broke his heart. Not long before that, Shea had had a close friend's mother pass away from cancer. A few weeks later, Rhonda asked Shea, "Do you worry about me?" He replied, "Mom, every day."

DEALING WITH THE DIAGNOSIS

The next step was to start treatment, which would not allow Rhonda the energy nor time to teach for the remainder of the school year. At the time, she had a student teacher, who would be put in an accelerated course and be taking over Rhonda's Spanish classes.

Telling her principal and colleagues was difficult and emotional, but by far the hardest part was sharing the news with her students. Rhonda gathered all her students in a circle to share the unexpected and sad news. Both high school boys and girls had tears running down their faces. Many gave her hugs. Even former students, no longer studying Spanish, came in to visit and show their support. Her colleagues came out of the woodwork with a strong show of support for her. Almost like wildfire, news of Rhonda's condition spread throughout the community and the other schools where she'd taught over the years. She admitted, "I assumed people—students, colleagues, and parents—didn't have the time to care. What had I been missing or thinking?"

Weekly treatments started at the Mayo Clinic in Rochester, which is world renowned and considered one of the best hospitals in the country and the world. However, it was a little over an hour drive from West Salem. On her first visit, the Mayo hematologist gave her hope. "Rhonda, this isn't a death sentence. There are many meds that can help with this."

The treatment prescribed was a multi-pronged approach. First, she would undergo two types of chemotherapy and finally an antibody treatment, Darzalex, which is an injection in the stomach. Every week, the treatment wiped her out. Rhonda found the most comfort in her living room recliner.

OUTPOURING OF SUPPORT

Every week for the rest of the year, parents, students, and family members sent Rhonda cards, letters, handmade gifts, gift cards, and Facebook messages. Her colleagues created a meal sign-up, and staff brought Rhonda and her family meals for several months. Plus, her student teacher organized a t-shirt campaign that said, "Cancer No Bueno – Viva McGowan." Many students and staff bought them and gave Rhonda the money from the sales. With this outpouring of love and support, Rhonda shares, "In a sense, I got to attend my own funeral and hear what people thought of me. It was pretty amazing and lifted me up in ways I can't explain."

Through this experience, Rhonda took on a new perspective. "I really relate to *Look Up*. It's not being depressed about what you're going through. Looking up to me means taking on a new perspective, looking up and around, *not* down—and one doesn't have to do it all on their own." For example, on a walk through a local park, Rhonda experienced a son-teaching-mother moment, including a dose of *Look Up*. Keegan was home for holiday leave from the Navy. At this time, Rhonda was having treatments and couldn't walk much because of bouts of nausea and breathlessness. Keegan wrapped his arm around her and said, "Mom, today is a bad day, but tomorrow will be a good day." Since childhood, he had always looked for the bright side of things, Rhonda shared.

After two and a half years of various treatments at Mayo and locally, Rhonda received the best gift anyone could ask for: She was declared officially in remission as of July 2021. Thus, she returned to the Spanish classroom, but she passed the baton of many of her leadership roles to another teacher.

The damage to her heart and colon couldn't be reversed. However, Rhonda's new normal included weightlifting and light cardio such as walking and snowshoeing. She had some persistent symptoms, including spots around her eyes and weight fluctuations—thus, the need for diuretics. However, with her second chance at life, Rhonda said, "Life is short. I look up and around, helping others who need help and leaning on others when I need to."

At the time of writing, Rhonda found out that she was no longer in remission. She was diagnosed with multiple myeloma, a plasma cancer closely related to AL. She has sought treatment and remains positive stating, "I'm still looking up and around."

ABOUT RHONDA MCGOWAN

Rhonda McGowan currently resides in West Salem, Wisconsin, with her husband of thirty years. Her two sons are now ages twenty-six and twenty-three. The youngest is still in the Navy.

Rhonda is a graduate of Arizona State University and has a master's degree from Nova Southeastern University in Spanish Language Education. She taught Spanish at the secondary level for thirty-two years and had also taught Spanish Methods for teachers at Viterbo University. As of 2023, she is retired but still subs in Spanish.

Rhonda also proudly speaks about the incurable disease of amyloidosis for the Amyloidosis Speakers Bureau, which serves medical schools and their students and residents. Her goals include enjoying life to the fullest with her husband, flying to visit their two sons in Texas and Seattle and traveling to Spanish-speaking countries.

PART 4:

FROM ADVERSITY TO PERSONAL EMPOWERMENT

BEING IN THE MOMENT —SAILING TO FRENCH POLYNESIA

HEIDI LOVE

Hiding out in a library, alone on a rainy night, fifteen-year-old Heidi Love discovered a copy of *National Geographic*. She turned to an article about the artist Paul Gauguin and his depictions of women and nature in French Polynesia. Looking to escape her day-to-day life in Pennsylvania, she gravitated to a picture of a beautiful waterfall. Her eyes moved down the page, landing on the caption, which read the "Bay of Virgins."

When recalling that moment, Heidi said, "That picture lit up the sky. I felt a jolt of energy course through me." On that library floor, Heidi's dream was born of not just traveling to French Polynesia but sailing there.

This dream of sailing to an unknown paradise was a way to break away from her traumatized and unsettled reality. After surviving rape and attempted murder at the age of eleven in Philadelphia, Heidi was prone to running away. Often, she came home only because the police found her. With time and much thought, her father hoped that distance away from where her horrific event happened would be therapeutic. Thus, the following summer, Heidi, age twelve, moved to her grandmother's empty cottage in New Jersey, which she would repeat for various summers to come. That first summer, her father gave Heidi a twelve-foot sailfish, which ignited her passion for sailing. During this time, she spread her wings of independence by learning sailing basics and waiting tables at a local restaurant.

A HEALTHY ESCAPE

During her first summer away, her family relocated from the inner city of Philly to the suburbs to further heal them all. It was there that the *National Geographic* article sparked her dream, coupled with the summers in New Jersey sailing. She recalls, "It was this dream that helped me survive." In essence, it was a healthy escape. The planning kept her sane and inspired her.

Fueling Heidi's passion, her tenth-grade biology teacher assigned her to read about Darwin. Heidi was fascinated by his stop in the Galapagos Islands and wanted to know how she could live in a place with seals, sea lions, turtles, and other marine wonders. She crafted a letter to the Ecuadorian government inquiring how she could live in the Galapagos. The response she received steered her studies. She could live in Galapagos, replied a government official, if she was born Ecuadorian, married an Ecuadorian, or was a marine biologist. The first two options were out—so Heidi graduated high school and eventually college with a degree in marine biology. To complement that degree, Heidi honed her nautical skills throughout her twenties. She crewed on boats, first in the Atlantic and later in the Caribbean and Mediterranean.

However, Heidi's adult life eventually got busier after college. She worked as a biology teacher in Europe, married, and had a son. Life seemed fairly normal, yet the trauma of her rape and strangulation had never disappeared. It was with her every day; but being a working mom took precedence over dealing with her emotions.

PTSD

After her son was born, Heidi and her husband divorced. The fear of being on her own and anxiety about possibly being raped again, triggered a first set of dissociative PTSD episodes where she would lose all sense of who or where she was. Later, when her son reached age eleven, the same age she had been when she experienced her trauma, her PTSD returned. A repeat vision would appear with her PTSD attacks. She would see her attacker's terrifying eyes and forget who she was. Wisely, Heidi chose to go to counseling to uncover the many layers of trauma she had repressed for decades. Once again, little by little, life became manageable. Using mindfulness techniques brought Heidi into the present instead of being drawn into the past.

A NEW MARRIAGE AND NEW ADVENTURE

After her divorce, Heidi began to thrive, and she successfully cofounded a marketing and design firm. She also created a profile on Match.com and found her now husband, Dennis. Heidi recalls, "When I met Dennis, it was similar to seeing that picture of the Polynesian waterfall. I felt unexplained electric energy course through my body." Dennis and Heidi were both business owners in their fifties who liked to sail. They eventually sold their home and bought a monohull sailboat named *Centime* (French for a cent, reminding sailors that little things matter). She asked Dennis, "Where do you want to sail?" and he tossed the same question back to her. The intended destination for one of their early voyages was none other than the Bay of Virgins in French Polynesia, a five-year, 12,000-nautical-mile feat and her lifelong dream.

Their voyage began with unexpected challenges and encounters. Upon sailing from Maine to the Caribbean with Dennis, Heidi thought she was healed from her past trauma, but she wasn't. On a brutal passage across the Gulf Stream, *Centime* was in the midst of an unexpected lightning storm. Heidi's fear brought on a surprise PTSD episode, complete with visions of her attacker.

She realized that while her assailant had attacked her once, she was reliving the attack thousands of times. In a way, her mind was perpetuating the attack. Time and time again, she couldn't stop her reaction to the fears and stressors of the trip.

Heidi had a decision to make. She knew that every sailor needs to be able to react and be in the moment to handle life-threatening conditions at sea. If she continued the voyage, she would endanger her life as well as Dennis's. When they reached the Panama Canal, Heidi chose to quit.

HEALING THERAPIES

Dennis and Heidi returned to Maine, but the dream to reach French Polynesia remained. Heidi sought the help of two courageous women: one a therapist who had climbed to 24,000 feet, near the "Death Zone" of Mount Everest, and another the captain of a sailing vessel that had circumnavigated the globe twice with all-female crews. The therapist was instrumental in teaching Heidi that no one can control the trigger to PTSD, but they can control their *reaction* to the trigger through mindfulness exercises. Heidi created a book of these exercises and developed a mind-balancing practice that greatly reduced her fear.

In 2012, Heidi and Dennis embarked once again on their journey to French Polynesia. Armed with not only the techniques of her therapist but some of her own, Heidi was more confident in her ability to control her reaction to stress. She explained, "If you're experiencing PTSD, you're not in the present. By developing a calming practice with breathing, meditation, music, mantras, or other mindful acts, you can learn to balance your emotional response to fear or anxiety and stay in the present." She added, "I had to learn how to defuse my emotions and later resolve them or I wouldn't have survived."

Thankfully, not all moments on that voyage were stressful; some were surprising and quite humorous. On a multi-day stop in the Galapagos, Heidi was dressed in a black, sea-lion-like wetsuit to go snorkeling in the cold waters. Almost instantly upon entering the water, she spotted a beautiful, young sea turtle but was intercepted by a massive mama sea turtle that clearly didn't want her near her offspring. Heidi splashed around to move back, which attracted a sea lion's attention. This curious sea lion circled her legs. Then he swam up her front side and backside, pressing his body against hers in a courting fashion. As she popped out of the water with her snorkel mask on, they stared at each other, both rather surprised. She suspects that the frisky male sea lion thought she was a female sea lion until that moment. What gave her away?

Her snorkel and mask didn't fit the sea lion mold. Swimming with a sea lion, interested or not, certainly put Heidi in the moment.

LAUGH AT THE SKY

During the three-week passage from the Galapagos Islands to French Polynesia, Heidi and Dennis were in the middle of the Pacific, one thousand miles away from land in every direction. Heidi was on night watch through a major squall while Dennis was sleeping below. Powerful nine-foot waves were crashing, colliding and creating fifteen-foot breaking waves that came from a dangerous direction. A forceful fifteen-foot breaker knocked the wind vane off course, making the boat turn rapidly upwind. Heidi knew that if the boom and sail dropped into the water, it would knock the boat all the way over, 360 degrees. She recounts, "My fear triggered an intense vision. I saw my assailant's glasses. Immediately, I tapped into the techniques. I took charge, turned the wheel, and steered the boat out of its precarious position. I raged at the waves instead of being afraid." The boat was still being hit by the wave trains, but at a better angle, back on course. This was definitely a moment that made Heidi *Look Up*.

In recounting her story, Heidi shared one of her favorite Buddhist sayings: "When you realize how perfect everything is, you will tilt your head back and laugh at the sky." She explains that, at first, this was difficult for her to understand. How can anything be perfect? When you've survived rape and attempted murder, when your marriage falls apart, when you're in a life-threatening storm, when you're alone experiencing dissociative PTSD, . . . how can you laugh at the sky? Yet when you're focused on the present, everything can be perfect in that moment—being able to see the sky, breathe air, feel the wind on your cheeks, or simply know you are alive. Laughing at the sky is finding the upside of the situation even if it's only from taking a single conscious breath. Perhaps that's a Buddhist way of saying *Look Up*.

Despite the challenges, Heidi and Dennis continued their journey. To find out if Heidi made it to French Polynesia or found that inspirational waterfall, check out her memoir,

Laughing at the Sky. And if you or someone you love is looking for greater emotional balance in life or support for living bold dreams, grab a copy of her *Knowing Acts—Engage in Healing,* a customizable workbook for emotional balance endorsed by a Harvard MD. Then, *Look Up* and laugh at the sky!

ABOUT HEIDI LOVE

Heidi Love is a sailor, activist, and author, as well as cofounder of Ethos Marketing *(ethosmarketing.com).* She graduated from the Institute for Civic Leadership and earned an MBA and Women of Achievement Fellowship from the University of New Hampshire. She's the author of *Laughing at the Sky—Wild Adventure, Bold Dreams, and a Daring Search for a Stolen Childhood,* her acclaimed memoir, which she wrote to inspire women on journeys of self-discovery. She's also the author of *Knowing Acts—Engage in Healing,* a customizable workbook and calming practice for emotional balance.

To connect with or learn more about Heidi Love, visit *www.heidiloveauthor.com.*

LOOK UP IN SPITE OF FEARS

RIDHISH DADBHAWLA

It was April 2003 when MBA university student Ridhish Dadbhawla left his cousin's family home in New Jersey. He started early in the morning for his new internship. His cousin kindly dropped Ridhish off at the closest train station. Then, Ridhish took a train into Manhattan and walked nearly an hour to the United Nations. He was anxious because it was his first time in the U.S., not to mention New York City and the United Nations. He recalled how his mother had urged him to take the internship despite their finances. "This is your golden opportunity," she had said to encourage him. "You are doing so well. Don't worry about the money."

LOSS AND CHALLENGE

Rewind to several years earlier in Mumbai, India, when Ridhish's father passed away of meningitis, in only his early forties. This left Ridhish, ten at the time, his younger sister, and their mother to create a new life. His father had been the sole breadwinner as a businessman, specializing in imports and exports. His passing was not only a tremendous emotional loss, but Ridhish's mother now needed to find a way to financially sustain her family. She had already completed high school before getting married but didn't get accepted into medical school; so instead, she dedicated herself to her family and raising her two children. At first, they got by with the financial help of good friends and family members. During this time, his mother tried several avenues to earn a livelihood for the family, always ensuring that the children had sufficient personal attention and care from her. Then, her luck changed. She landed a mathematics tutoring opportunity and eventually started a full-time business tutoring kids.

Losing his father and seeing his mother reinvent herself was a turning point for Ridhish. He came from humble beginnings, but he realized that with higher education, he could rise up and prevent this from happening to his family ever again.

OUT OF HIS COMFORT ZONE INTO THE FIRE

At the end of his undergrad studies in India and without a father figure, Ridhish looked to his uncle, who had moved to the U.S., as a mentor. After working at a prestigious college in Mumbai, his uncle was now a CFO in a U.S. tech company. At the time,

Ridhish was an introvert and an average student. He didn't know what career path to take. His uncle wisely suggested he apply for an MBA. Fortunately, Ridhish was accepted, but he shared, "I was out of my comfort zone. I was going to have to force myself to present projects, network, and be more outgoing."

In his first year at his business school, a speaker from the United Nations' Department of Economic and Social Affairs came to speak to the student body and faculty. Little did Ridhish know how much this presentation from Hanifa Mezoui would change his life course. During her time at the college, Hanifa explained her department's project helping international NGOs (Non-Governmental Organizations with social aims). Through a bi-yearly meeting at the United Nations in New York, nineteen dignitaries from across the globe evaluate the NGOs, providing a seal of U.N. approval to validate the status of the NGOs that qualify. At the time, all the applications and supporting documents were paper. All were translated into six different languages and organized into binders. It took a team of interns nearly four months to organize all the paperwork and binders. Seeing the need for digital evolution, the dean of the MBA school told Hanifa, "Our students can help deploy a paperless office."

In 2003, the United Nations (UN) launched its internship program to create a paperless office. The job would involve a two-month internship in New York, starting in April 2003. The bad news? Neither the school nor the UN would pay for travel, food, and lodging.

With encouragement from his mother, Ridhish applied and went through a strenuous, multiple-interview process that evaluated his presentation skills, grooming, and technology skills. Luckily, Ridhish was selected as one of nine from a total of 250 other students at his Mumbai business school. The other eight were great at presentations and communication in general, but Ridhish was the only one with skills in technology, having taken various computer courses. In fact, since graduating from high school, Ridhish had been tutoring students in computer fundamentals and Microsoft Office applications for a source of income.

Before leaving India for the States, the team of interns went through a lot of preparatory training materials sent by the UN. One of the most complex pieces of the paperless office endeavor was to set up a Wi-Fi network. At the time, Wi-Fi was a relatively new technology, and most of all networks were wired. Ridhish led the team through the setup as the tech expert—but what technology challenges lay ahead in The Big Apple?

MULTIPLE ADJUSTMENTS

On his first day, Ridhish was not only adjusting to a new country, a cold climate, the grandness of New York, and the United Nations, but he was the lone technology expert on the team of nine. After Hanifa welcomed all to the team, she passed the baton to the UN's IT lead Daniel Perez and deputy Meena Sur. Daniel addressed the interns: "We're trying to build an intranet portal and we're going to scan all the documents.

We've partnered with HP, and they're providing laptops, routers, modems, scanners, and printers." Basically, Ridhish and the other interns were part of the pilot program for a paperless office for the entire UN.

This wasn't a typical first day where you learn where your desk and the coffee maker are located. This was a timebound DIY project. Before lunch break, the other interns were instructed to oversee Plan B, the old-school paper option of organizing binders. That left Ridhish to work on Plan A. As the others left for lunch, Daniel led Ridhish over to a large scanner and printer—something Ridhish had never seen before. Looking at Ridhish, Daniel told him, "You need to activate this machine, configure it, and set it up."

Not without hiccups, Ridhish discovered how to do all the above, but that was just the tip of the iceberg. He needed to deploy technology, including setting up servers and Wi-Fi throughout the conference rooms and troubleshoot any technology failures. Once Ridhish deemed the system ready, the fellow interns trained the dignitaries. It was like a dress rehearsal for the evaluation day.

BIG PROBLEM

After a successful training with the dignitaries, the NGO evaluation day came. All the dignitaries had a laptop. At the commencement of the meeting, the technology failed. What worked in dress rehearsal did *not* on the big day. This quickly put Plan B into effect, utilizing the binders.

Ridhish rushed into the server room with only one thing on his mind: Solve this problem. Shortly, he determined that a server had backfired, and he needed to check the connections between the routers. Then, he powered the system off and on.

Upon rebooting, everything seemed functional. In this moment of immense pressure, Ridhish walked forward and *looked up* in spite of his fears to suggest that Meena and Daniel resume Plan A. Reluctantly, they did, afraid the dignitaries would lose patience with the project. However, it worked then and for the entire week. At the end of this monumental week, the intern team received not only a standing ovation from the dignitaries but coveted UN awards as well as an invitation to the Indian ambassador's home. This was a tremendous accolade and experience for all the interns, but especially for young Ridhish.

When looking back on how this achievement changed his life, he admitted, "I never thought I could've solved these problems. The UN experience made me more resourceful. It boosted my confidence. Things seemed hard," Ridhish added, "but putting my best foot forward did the trick."

In essence, by focusing on the task at hand or in the moment, all of us can accomplish more than we might have thought. Plus, by tapping into the power of perspective and the success of past struggles, we can find the upside to any situation.

SUCCESS LEADS TO MORE SUCCESS—AND HAPPINESS

After the rewarding experience in New York City, Ridhish returned to Mumbai to finish his MBA. Unlike his beginning in post-graduate school, Ridhish was no longer afraid to present projects. Also, his academic performance was top of the class. In fact, he received the Best Student award and coverage in leading Indian newspapers alongside other interns. "I was a different person after the UN," he reported. He graduated with an MBA, specializing in finance.

Soon after graduation, Ridhish landed employment with PwC (PricewaterhouseCoopers) as a management consultant in tax advisory, followed by a job as a senior technology consultant at IBM. This position was based in India but allowed frequent travel to Europe and other parts of the world. During this time, Ridhish met his now wife, Shivani, through a traditional arranged marriage. They married in India and shortly after moved to New Jersey for Ridhish's career.

Neither Shivani nor Ridhish liked the cold, so they relocated to California. Presently, Ridhish lends his expertise to the largest consulting company in the world, Accenture. Also, he and Shivani have two children, a boy and a girl. His wife has contributed to his success by always being a true partner in his personal and professional goals. Ridhish imparts the following about his journey: "I feel blessed that my destiny, my mother's perseverance, and my wife's love and unconditional support gave me the chance to prove myself. Each step gave me the courage to pursue further goals. Even today, my family is instrumental in giving me the will power to explore unchartered territories, which has always helped me in my journey. Don't give up; keep moving and look up!"

ABOUT RIDHISH DADBHAWALA

Ridhish Dadbhawala is a seasoned leader experienced in transforming and managing digital systems. His diverse experience of working with topnotch brands such as Nike, Boeing, Sony Music, and Autodesk has contributed to his versatility in solving challenging problems. He has managed large cross-functional teams, driving complex transformations to scale businesses to double-digit revenue.

Ridhish's wife Shivani has an MS in Child Psychology and is an early childhood educator by profession. Outside of work, the two of them love playing board games and biking with their children, Vihaan and Riya. Ridhish's mother enjoys spending time with her grandchildren and loves teaching them mathematics. His younger sister became a Human Resources professional and settled in Sydney, Australia, with her family.

HOUSE OF CARDS
DR. BROOKE FOREMAN

Brooke and John, both in their mid-forties, had everything: fancy clothes, houses, boats, cars, and events to attend. John was a VP at a world-renowned manufacturer in Austin, Texas, and frequently traveled internationally. Brooke was an acupuncturist with an OB/GYN degree, not because she needed the money, but because of a passion to help others with Eastern medicine. Brooke shared, "Our life consisted of John traveling around the world for work with me occasionally accompanying him to fabulous places and attending dinners as an interesting trophy wife. I was a real-life Austin 'housewife.'"

SHELL SHOCK

Everything was going along as usual, until one day after John had left on another business trip. Brooke was doing her morning routine, when she was interrupted by various text messages on John's iPad. He had forgotten it in the rush to get to the airport. Although the iPad was locked, Brooke could read the incoming messages before they faded away. They weren't work related. On the contrary, the messages were to set up a romantic rendezvous. The texts continued with more and more graphic details. Ping after ping, she discovered the unfathomable. John was not setting up a booty call with another woman but with a man, or more accurately, men. The graphic messages weren't coordinating a date with a romantic partner. They mentioned more detailed escapades, such as blindfolded parking-lot meetups, French-maid-costume hotel hookups, and even gay bars with glory hole encounters (Google that if you don't know what those are). He was John Doe-ing around the world quite literally. Brooke recounted, "I sat in the kitchen shell shocked. I needed to find out more!"

Without knowing John's passcode, she took a deep breath, typed in her best guess, and held her breath. BAM, it opened! Brooke dove into his personal email where she began to uncover all the lies he, she, and they were living. Scouring as far back as she could, Brooke discovered that John had been with countless men around the world on highly X-rated, one-time-only encounters. "All of a sudden what I thought was true was not. I was knocked into being fully conscious. I flipped off autopilot and turned on being in the moment," Brooke remembered.

Not knowing what their future would hold, she forwarded all emails and racy pictures to her account. However, she didn't stop with his sexual betrayal. Brooke's instincts told her there were *additional* falsehoods to John's deceitful life. The more she dug into his past, the more lies she unearthed. John had been pulling the wool over everyone's eyes for a long time. For one thing, he had never graduated from the University of Texas or played baseball there.

He had falsified his resume, lying to his employer for over seventeen years. Cheating on his wife with a multitude of men and being a fraud at work were depraved, but Brooke uncovered one of the worst lies of them all; he had told Brooke and many others that he had cancer. This lie coincided with that year's Formula 3 powerboat racing season, in which he was racing. The event press got wind of his illness and John became the media darling—on purpose. No lie was too big or too low for John.

DETERMINING AND EXECUTING A PLAN

Instead of confronting John about all of this, she decided to share her story with a select few lifelong friends, clients, and colleagues, who quickly became angels in Brooke's story. Tere, a successful career woman and client of Brooke's, suggested a much-needed getaway. Tere was recovering from cancer, so John's unscrupulous lie about the Big C boiled her blood. Coincidentally, Tere and her best friend were going to Kauai for a girls' getaway in a few weeks. Tere invited Brooke to come along and stay with them, no charge. Brooke took that very same iPad and booked a ticket to Kauai.

Her plan was to keep everything at home copacetic, which was harder than she thought. She would hold on to what she knew and do her due diligence until another of John's trips to tell him she wanted a divorce. Then, while he was away, she'd pack up precious things and her dog Aruba and escape to Kauai for a needed reset.

Knowing John wouldn't take the divorce news lightly, Brooke decided to break her silence in public. She did the wifely thing and drove John to the Austin airport for his next trip. Upon saying goodbye outside of the SUV, she asked him for a strong hug and then for a divorce. In a rush for a very important presentation, John was ambushed. He couldn't cancel his travel plans last minute nor make a scene at the airport for security and others to witness. Brooke quickly left and drove home to pack her things and get her dog, not answering the incessant phone calls and texts from John. While she was clearing out her essentials in the walk-in closet, she stumbled across a French maid outfit, which fueled her fire to get out of Austin and off to Hawaii. She dropped the dog off with her parents and continued to Dallas to hop a flight to Lihue, Kauai.

Known as a special place with incredible healing powers, Kauai was just what Brooke needed. With the strong, wise advice of Tere and her best friend, Brooke realized it would be dangerous to have any contact with John. He was a sociopath who had no empathy. She was the only one who knew all his lies. Brooke had the power to destroy his house of cards. So, she formulated her next plan. Upon her return, she would hide out at Tere's house until the divorce was finalized.

Back in Austin, John still wanted control over Brooke; thus, he dragged out the divorce process. During this time, Brooke's attorney joked, "I should get a bottle of wine and some popcorn and read the myriad rendezvous emails with graphic photos for a nightly dose of an Austin-based reality show." They both chuckled about the "entertainment" value of the emails.

The attorney happily forwarded Brooke's bills to John. When John learned that because Texas was a Community Property state, he had to pay not only his lawyer's fees but hers as well, John quickly signed the papers so as not to prolong the process further.

Although their lives had looked ritzy on the outside, with fancy cars, homes, boats, clothes, and events, their lifestyle was heavily supported by credit cards, which meant more debt than money. Therefore, Brooke's divorce settlement was only a portion of John's 401K, which she couldn't touch, and enough money to get herself back on her feet somewhere for roughly three months.

A NEW LIFE—GUESS WHERE

Brooke had a choice: to reboot and start life afresh in Austin or restart life someplace new. Growing up in Iowa, she knew cold weather wasn't going to do. She thought a warm place where she could live and eventually retire would be ideal. Her first thought was Florida. In fact, she received a job offer at a prominent medical clinic on Sanibel Island in Florida. She basically accepted it but told the supervisor that she wanted to sleep on it. That very night, she dreamed of Kauai and its splendor: sacred forests, waterfalls, the NaPali Coast, and Waimea Canyon, the Grand Canyon of the Pacific.

The very next day, she said no to the job offer and secretly started selling her possessions and planning her move. She knew that others would try to convince her to stay or move to Florida, so she said nothing, even to her parents, until seven days prior to moving.

When asked about her connection to *Look Up,* Brooke commented, "My story abruptly threw me into the present moment. I was letting someone else drive my life. Now, I live consciously." She added, "I think life is about these times that we step up and learn more about ourselves. I never would have left my cushy life if none of this horrible shit had happened to me. What sounds like a Dateline episode led to my dream life. I'm so grateful."

In Kauai, she focused her new life on conscious living and being in the moment. She began teaching yoga and meditation classes at the Marriott in Lihue. Instead of throwing her wedding ring into the ocean upon arrival, she sold it and used the funds to earn her doctorate in acupuncture. Dr. Brooke has since opened an acupuncture clinic in Kapa'a, offers online programs for women's health and empowerment, and continues to teach wellness classes.

ABOUT DR. BROOKE FOREMAN

Dr. Brooke Foreman is a former pharmaceutical sales representative turned Eastern medicine doctor. She stands strong for women having vibrancy throughout their life. As a women's beauty and vitality expert, she pulls from her passions in Eastern and functional medicine, natural skincare, fitness, and yoga to serve her patients.

During her more than twenty-five years of healthcare experience, she has been called a "miracle worker," "Dr. Sunshine," and "wellness warrior" by patients and colleagues. Why? Because she's a relentless fighter for her patients, investigating and delivering the best, simplest, and safest ways to improve their lives as quickly as possible. She has inspired and empowered thousands of clients, instructors, healthcare providers, and patients worldwide by integrating the best of Eastern and Western, scientifically-sound healing modalities for beauty and longevity. Visit her website at *www. brookeforeman.com.*

FROM ADVERSITY
TO PURPOSE

TOM THIBODEAU

For over forty years, Tom Thibodeau has been teaching at Viterbo University, a private, Catholic Franciscan University in La Crosse, Wisconsin. For half of those years, he has specialized in servant leadership. For those unfamiliar with the term, servant leadership is a leadership approach in which the leader's primary focus is on serving others, making their needs and well-being a priority to help them grow and succeed. Tom started the servant leadership topic as a semester course. Then, it morphed into a certificate program. In 2001, it became a master's program. Like other disciplines, Tom's courses require readings and lectures, but he also believes in experiential learning.

One of his most powerful activities is having students spend a cold February night sitting outside in a lawn chair, experiencing just a fraction of what it feels like to be homeless. The students are required to stay out all night, feeling the chill seep into their bones, with no shelter, no warmth—just the raw, biting cold of a Wisconsin winter. The next day, they're expected to go about their regular schedule, attending classes and trying to focus while grappling with the effects of a sleepless, freezing night.

Tom explains how this experience can affect his students: "You can *talk* about being homeless, you can *discuss* displacement and loneliness, but nothing teaches compassion like sitting in the cold for twelve hours and then having to go to class the next day. That's when it hits them: *Would I want to do this every night?*" This immersive experience shifts the students' perspectives, allowing them to build empathy and understanding for the struggles of those they are learning to serve.

INSPIRED BY SERVICE AND LOVE

Many ask why Tom has dedicated most of his professional and personal life to servant leadership. To get to the bottom of Tom's why, he preferred to explain through a story and suggested traveling back to the 1960s and his small town of Wisconsin Rapids.

At that time, the Thibodeaus were a family of seven, with another child on the way. Tom's father was a lawyer, and his mother tended to the five children. Three months into her pregnancy, the doctor advised her to remain on bed rest for the duration of the pregnancy. As a result, they relocated her bed to the living room, and from there she taught Tom, the eldest, how to cook, clean, and iron.

After the birth of their sixth child, Tom's mother went into a deep post-partum depression and was admitted to a psychiatric ward in Marshfield, a half-hour away from their hometown. With no relatives nearby, Tom's role became caring for his five younger siblings, which meant he needed to drop out of school when only in sixth grade.

Concerned about his mother, Tom asked his father, "Who's taking care of mother?" His father explained that psychologists and psychiatrists were caring for her. Tom felt compelled to become someone who could help serve his mother and people like her.

Upon her return home, after almost three months in the hospital, Tom's mother was not nearly able to care for six children while tending to cooking, cleaning, shopping, and everything else. Their neighbors, church members, and friends took the initiative to show up and step in. Every night without fail there was a meal on the kitchen table. Their community literally fed the Thibodeaus, the grandest of gestures. This experience of service and love sparked Tom's purpose when he was still only twelve. He wanted to serve others the way people had done for his family during this difficult time.

Well into his tenure at Viterbo, Tom returned home to visit his mother. She asked, "Tom, why are you doing what you're doing?" He jokingly answered, "I like to talk." She didn't care much for the joke and commented, "When you were growing up, I wasn't the mother you needed, nor the one I wanted to be." She reflected on the times when Tom had to take on responsibilities such as make breakfast and take care of his siblings while she struggled with depression. She admitted that many days she couldn't get out of her housecoat and would just sit on the couch and cry. Despite this, she prayed every day for her children to follow the path God intended for them. Tom reassured her that he was using his gifts, which were leading him to his purpose of serving others.

When asked to describe himself, Tom shared, "I'm an ambassador for goodness. I try to create levels of hospitality, communities, where people can experience one another as guests, as friends, and as neighbors. Hospitality is an oasis from hostility." He continued to highlight that "Welcoming someone is an ancient gift. In all cultures, they always consider hospitality—the way you treat your guests. It's very important to realize that often it's the most hospitable people who are those with the least. All of a sudden that hospitality becomes a gift of self."

CONNECTION TO THE LOOK UP MANTRA

To gift *yourself,* you must be in the moment and be present—and that's one of Tom's connections to the *Look Up* mantra. He believes that if people feel welcome, it creates common ground. He adds that the great malady of our culture is loneliness. That's why hospitality is so necessary for all of us. He commented, "So many people are hungry, but it's not just for bread. It's for community, a place to gather at a common table. Let's be guests in each other's lives, not adversaries. Good people do good things together."

His connection to *Look Up* also speaks to the idea that service is love made visible—every act of service, no matter how small an expression of love it is. Tom shared this Rabbi Heschel quote: "Above all, remember that you must build your life as if it were a work of art."

Tom coupled that with, "This should be where each action, each decision, and each relationship is crafted with care, intention, and love." His approach involves being mindful of how you spend your time, how you interact with others, and how you contribute to the world around you. In essence, be kind and look up.

ABOUT TOM THIBODEAU

Tom is a proud husband, father, grandfather, and active community member. He also holds countless accolades, titles, and degrees. In 2023, he celebrated twenty years since the first cohort of servant leadership grad students completed their studies. In addition, Tom is an inspirational speaker on servant leadership, giving nearly a hundred talks and workshops a year across the country and internationally. Find out more in Tom's TEDx Talk on YouTube.

PAIN WITH A PURPOSE: CREATING A MEANINGFUL MOSAIC

KRYSTLE KNIGHT

In 2020 in Grundy County, Tennessee, between Nashville and Chattanooga, Krystle was married to her husband Bill, with whom she had two boys, six and eleven. In addition, they were raising two children from her previous relationships, a fourteen-year-old boy and a nineteen-year-old young woman. Krystle, like much of the workforce that year, found herself laid off because of the COVID-19 pandemic.

Since early adolescence, Krystle had a past of using methamphetamines and alcohol. She shares, "Twenty-four years of my life were a rebellion and a blur because of drugs and alcohol." She admits that in her marriage with Bill, Krystle wasn't doing meth, but she and Bill were both alcoholics, living in a toxic relationship marred by physical abuse. "There were black eyes, shattered dishes, and holes in the walls," she says.

With the combination of stressors, Krystle found herself increasingly consumed by addiction. Following a violent altercation with her husband, she tried to flee the fight and got into her Toyota Camry and ran into Bill with the car, which resulted in an aggravated assault arrest. Sitting in the back of the cop car, she decided to leave him; but instead of seeking stability, she spiraled downward. "I made a conscious decision to run wild," she admits. "I told myself, 'What's the harm?'"

RUNNING WILD AND HITTING BOTTOM

Krystle's rebellion led her to the streets and staying with drug-related friends and associates. She bounced between the homes of acquaintances and hotels, living a nomadic existence across Tennessee and Georgia, seeking shelter in the underground drug network. Arrested multiple times for various charges, she needed to be monitored by the State of Tennessee. She was given a GPS bracelet, which along the way she decided to cut off, and after that, she lived in a constant state of fear and survival. "I was living out of my car, trying to stay one step ahead of the law," she recalls.

The tipping point came in the fall of 2020. Krystle had fled to Georgia and was staying at a stranger's house. That stranger's adult children found out about this harboring of a possible convict, showed up demanding that she leave, and called the police. That night, Krystle left but didn't go far. She went to the nearest gas station and waited for the police to find her—a decision she still doesn't fully understand but now credits to divine intervention. When the officers arrived, she thanked them as they escorted her into the back of the car. "One officer said, 'I've never had anyone thank me for arresting them before,'" she remembers. "I told him, 'This is the help I need.'"

In the cop car on her way to the Whitfield County jail, she remembers the radio playing. The first song told the story that the beast you feed is the one that's in control. She realized that the way she'd been living was a combination of her choices, and it was time for a new start.

THE NASHVILLE RESCUE MISSION

After months in three county jails across two states, Krystle was offered a chance to join the Nashville Rescue Mission's women's program. She initially resisted. "I didn't think I needed it," she said. However, when she finally arrived, she was struck by the Mission's emblem: a heart with a cross, symbolizing hope. "It was like God saying, 'Do you see now?'"

The Nashville Rescue Mission provided not only room and board but also structure, work therapy, and emotional support.

Krystle found solace in its routine of daily chores, classes, and Bible studies.

Because she was coming from a life ruled by addiction, she had been in and out of jail, on the run, fighting others, and witnessing people dying around her. Krystle had been living in chaos and darkness. She didn't care if she needed to steal when hungry or lie to get want she wanted. She didn't have respect for herself nor anybody else. That's why the structure and training of the Nashville Rescue Mission was such a cornerstone of Krystle's journey. "They retrain your heart and mind," she explained. "It's like they pour love and discipline into you until you believe you're worth it."

Over six months, Krystle transformed. She learned to embrace accountability, rebuild her work ethic, and face her past with honesty. "I used to think I was broken," she said, "but the Mission taught me that even shattered pieces can become something beautiful."

FROM SURVIVAL TO SERVICE

After graduating from the program in July of 2021, Krystle was hired by the Mission as an operations specialist. Within months, she earned a promotion to operations coordinator. Today, she supervises women in the same program that saved her life, offering them hope and guidance. "I tell them, 'If I can do it, you can too,'" she says. "I've been where you are. I know what it's like to think there's no way out."

Krystle's personal life has also flourished. She is now married to Kyle, a fellow graduate of the Mission's program. Together, they've built a stable life, complete with a home, a car, and meaningful work. Krystle's relationships with her children and parents are restored, a testament to the healing power of time and effort. "It's not perfect," she says, "but it's a far cry from how I used to live."

LOOK UP AND SEE YOUR MOSAIC

Krystle's story is deeply connected to the theme of *Look Up*. She describes her transformation as finding the "new-start button" and choosing to press it. "During my last bottom, I kept seeing signs, such as arrows, hearts, messages of hope," she said. "They reminded me to keep going."

Her journey from addiction to joy has taught her profound lessons about resilience and perspective. "There's always hope," she affirms. "Even when you think you've hit your last bottom, there's a way up. You just have to look for the road signs."

One metaphor Krystle often shares with the women she mentors is that of the mosaic. "Life can shatter you," she says, "but those broken pieces can be rearranged into something more beautiful and impactful than before."

THE GIFT OF GIVING BACK

Today, Krystle's life is a testament to the power of second chances. At the Mission, she helps women who remind her of her past self. "Every time I see one of them graduate, it's like a piece of my heart heals," she says.

For Krystle, the joy of her current stage of life isn't just in her own recovery but in the opportunity to guide others. "This is my purpose," she declares. "It's to show others that no matter how tough, dark, and bad it gets, there's always a way to start over."

Krystle's story is one of resilience and the transformative power of hope. It's a reminder to all of us to look up, even in our scariest hours, and find the courage to restart.

ABOUT KRYSTLE KNIGHT

Krystle Knight is a mother, wife, daughter, friend, and mentor to many. She is a Tennessee native who currently hangs her hat with her husband Kyle in Nashville. Both are graduates of the Nashville Rescue Mission and have worked at the Mission for several years. Krystle lives a sober lifestyle with the goal to turn her hard lessons into inspiration to help other women at the Nashville Rescue Mission to restart with a meaningful life and to flourish. To learn more about the Nashville Rescue Mission, visit *www.nashvillerescuemission.org*.

FOLLOWING THE INDIGO THREAD

ANDREW KRICHELS

Born into a privileged family in the Berkshires of western Massachusetts, Andrew was the youngest boy of six children. His father was a German aristocrat who had left Europe during World War II and started a successful papermill business near Stockbridge. His mother was a professional classical pianist from a well-known, respected New England family from Boston. The Krichels were high society, entertaining the likes of Ted Shaw and Joseph Pilates, while the kids studied at the best boarding schools and continued with Ivy League educations. However, Andrew's early years were a paradox. "It was idyllic if you didn't look under the surface." Andrew recounts, beneath the surface, his childhood was riddled with trauma, including sexual abuse and the early deaths of both parents.

His father's sudden death from a heart attack when Andrew was just nine years old was the first fracture in the veneer of their privileged life. A year later, his mother developed cancer and discovered a love for alcohol. By this time, his other siblings were already out of the house. So, from sixth grade through high school, Andrew witnessed his mother in and out of hospitals and, when home, so intoxicated she couldn't make it to her own bedroom.

This environment led Andrew to rebel, turning to drugs, alcohol, and multiple sexual partners, both women and men. "Our house became an open den for kids experimenting with drugs," he said. "I thought I was being responsible by setting rules like 'no heroin in the front part of the house,' but it was madness." Deep down, Andrew's fear was that social services would take him away from their home if his mother passed before he could make it to eighteen. By chance, Andrew graduated high school and turned eighteen not long before his mother passed. Out of duty, her family made sure the six children went to college, but there was no large inheritance, and the home was sold quickly. As he put it, "The family pruned the tree—and swiftly."

DANCE: A LIFELINE AND AN IDENTITY

Despite his tumultuous childhood, Andrew discovered an early passion for movement and creativity as an escape. As young as ten years old, he would sneak into Tanglewood to listen to the Boston Symphony Orchestra and dance for hours. "My parents wanted me to be a lawyer or a politician," he shared. Growing up, it was okay for Andrew to take ballroom lessons, but dancing was not to be a career. "My father would say dance is good exercise."

After his parents' death, Andrew bummed around Europe with friends from the Berkshires. One pivotal night in Copenhagen, Andrew was walking the cobblestone streets when he heard drums. He followed the rhythm toward a window with a front-row view of an impromptu, avant-garde dance workshop. "Not shy, the dancers pulled me through a side window to watch and dance with them," he recalled. "From that moment, I knew dance was my path."

Andrew's talent and determination led him to train at the Boston Conservatory, where he met his wife Kathleen, and they both continued to study dance at SUNY Purchase. There, Andrew worked alongside luminaries such as Mark Morris and Bill T. Jones. Quickly, his career took off, and he became a celebrated figure in the New York dance scene, while traveling the globe with over fifteen dance companies. Yet, despite outward success, Andrew battled feelings of inadequacy rooted in childhood trauma. "I was listed among the top dancers," he said, "but I never felt completely accepted."

TURNING POINTS: THE CRASH AND THE MIRROR

The fast-paced world of professional dance came with its own perils. Immersed in the hedonistic culture of the 1980s, Andrew struggled with substance abuse and tumultuous relationships. As he half-jokingly described it, "I survived on the dancer diet: bourbon, cocaine, and cigarettes." With the euphoria of the nightly performance coupled with the stress and bodily injuries, Andrew needed more and more to feel good. At one point, he had arthritic feet, having broken them countless times, a severed shoulder, and a doctor's recommendation to fuse seven of his vertebrae.

Stuart, a peer dancer and Andrew's best friend, noticed the toxic behavior as all too familiar. Stuart was a recovering alcoholic and introduced Andrew to Alcoholics Anonymous (AA). Andrew wasn't ready when Stuart invited him to attend the meetings. It wasn't until years later and after Stuart's passing from AIDS that a moment of reckoning occurred.

In the early 1990s, Andrew got into a devastating car crash in upstate New York. Three drag racers struck the small car Andrew was driving, leaving him unconscious and with severe injuries. "I left my body during that crash," Andrew recalled. "Watching it all unfold from above was a spiritual wake-up call. It was as if life was telling me, 'Pay attention. There is something deeper you need to explore.'"

This was the first aha moment needed for Andrew to start adjusting course; he needed to heal himself without surgery, embracing techniques from his childhood such as Pilates, and studies from SUNY incorporating Eastern medicine, in particular qigong. Through his healing process, Andrew had an epiphany: "Movement is more than a performance; it can heal."

Healed enough to perform again, Andrew took the stage once more, but this time in Nashville. After the show, he went to a gay hustler bar in East Nashville. At nearly bar time, "I looked in the mirror," he said. "I still had mascara under my eyes from the show, my pants were ripped, my hair was slicked back, and I was holding a glass of Jack Daniels and a cigarette. That was reality. The truth staring back at me was unbearable." At the age of forty, that moment in the mirror propelled him to attend his first AA meeting. "I've been clean and sober for thirty-four years," he proudly stated.

With a new, defined course, Andrew made tough decisions: He and Kathleen divorced, and he moved to Nashville, Tennessee. He had been frequently visiting "Music City," helping Leonard Bernstein in his goal to establish a Leonard Bernstein Center for Education of the Arts. Living in East Nashville opened the door for Andrew to start the Tennessee Dance Theater alongside Donna Rizzo. Although the dance company traveled to New York and Paris and received great reviews, it never caught on in Nashville. Both projects eventually flopped; thus, all signs were pointing toward his new direction—how to share his learnings with others.

With new direction came new love. Nashville set the stage for meeting his new life partner, Bill, who was born and raised in Tennessee and is a well-known visual artist, working in stained glass and painting.

EMBRACING THE INDIGO THREAD

Throughout his life, Andrew followed what he calls the "Indigo Thread," a metaphor for his true essence and purpose. "Who is that essential person beneath the roles and traumas?" he mused. "The little boy dancing at Tanglewood, the man drawn through the window in Copenhagen—that's the thread that's carried me through everything."

Andrew credits his sobriety and spiritual exploration with helping him reconnect to this essence. He deepened his practice through studies in movement therapy and spirituality, culminating in a program at Naropa University in Boulder, Colorado. There, he developed a unique approach to healing that integrates the body, mind, and spirit. "It's always been through the body for me," he explained. "Movement holds the key to unlocking trauma and finding wholeness."

A LIFE OF SERVICE: HEALING THROUGH MOVEMENT

Today, Andrew dedicates his life to helping others overcome trauma and addiction. His workshops blend dance, meditation, and storytelling to create safe spaces for transformation. "Don't deny your story," he tells participants. "Own it and weave it into your cellular system. Think of it like a tapestry."

Andrew's work is deeply informed by his own journey. "When I first got sober, I wasn't looking for a Disney cartoon of happiness," he said. "I wanted to be fully human, to embrace the courage it takes to feel vulnerable and hurt without judgment."

THE LOOK UP MANTRA

Andrew's story aligns powerfully with the *Look Up* mantra, which emphasizes finding a lesson in every obstacle. "Every persona I built—the aristocrat's child, the celebrated dancer—crumbled over time," he reflected. "What remained was my Indigo Thread, the essence of who I am. Following that thread has led me to healing and to helping others heal."

One of Andrew's favorite assertions captures this philosophy: "The deeper you plié, the higher you jump." For him, life's challenges have become opportunities to grow. "There's a pattern to all of it," he said. "Surviving isn't enough. The real question is, how can I help others survive and thrive?"

Now Andrew continues to explore new chapters in his life. Based in Nashville, he remains a guide and mentor for those seeking to heal. He dreams of expanding his work and exploring new creative ventures. "There's always another chapter," he said. "The Indigo Thread hasn't led me astray yet."

ABOUT ANDREW KRICHELS

Andrew Krichels has developed Experiential Movement Therapy through a lifetime of experience, training, and passion for his core belief: Move the body and the mind will follow. His early training at The Boston Conservatory of Music and SUNY Purchase produced a joint degree in Dance and Psychology. Andrew went on to a successful twenty-five-year career, and taught on the faculties of the Lincoln Center, the Leonard Bernstein Center, and The Grammy Foundation.

Andrew has always had a fascination with human behavior and what motivates us to navigate life's challenges in a healing and effective way. Seeking relief from extreme dance injuries led him to advanced certifications in Pilates, Bowen Therapy, and Medical Qigong.

Connect to Andrew, his workshops, and his upcoming book through *www.creativeactionseminars.com.*

LIVING AUTHENTICALLY
THE FREDERICKS

In a quiet town on the Northern California coast, Nell, a high school junior, balances academics, athletics, and a close-knit group of friends. With her bold confidence and athletic skill, Nell shines as the goalie for the girls' soccer team, a role she cherishes with a competitive spark and deep pride. She shares the love of the sport and sports in general with her parents, Mark and Nina, as well as with her sister Wren, who plays on the team, too. Although her older brother Oliver is already in college, he recalls that Nell has always been gifted at athletics. For five summers in a row, all three siblings were on the road with their parents in a camper for Nell's traveling baseball league.

THE CHALLENGE

However, the journey to this point was neither straightforward nor easy. Just four years ago, in the winter of 2021, Nell's destiny began to take shape. At the time, she was still known as Ryan, a middle schooler grappling with questions of identity amidst the isolation of the pandemic. To get out of the house and burn off some of that youthful energy, she joined the cross-country team, where she met new friends who were also curious about their identity. Through Nell's new friends and school support, she joined a Gender-Sexuality Alliance (GSA) group online, which marked a turning point. Though she initially joined to support friends, it became a space where she could explore her own feelings. In fact, Nell and the members of the group nicknamed the group the Alphabet Mafia, a play on words for the LGBTQIA2S+ acronym.

TRANSITION TIME

Through exploration and learning, that spring Nell admitted to her parents that she was a pansexual, a person who feels attracted to individuals regardless of gender. She wanted to start socially transitioning in the house by way of manners, speech, and attire. Nell also began to transition around trusted friends outside of school. By the end of seventh grade, Nell emailed her teachers to announce her new name, Nell, and her pronouns. Most people would probably assume a preteen would consult with her parents first—but nope; she went ahead without telling her parents.

Her parents' reactions were layered with love, concern, and self-reflection. Both supported Nell from day one, but they feared how the rest of the world would treat their daughter. "I thought I was as liberal as they come," Nina admitted. "But having a trans child forced me to confront biases I didn't even know I had."

Nina and Mark shared one of the challenges they faced: "Parents agonize and dream of a good name before their children are born. It's not easy to let go of this as parents; however, it's part of the growing process in allowing these amazing individuals the freedom to become who they were always meant to be. We, as parents, have some influence, and we have some authority. But if we misplay our authority, we'll end up with less influence." This shaped much of all of their children's paths.

In seventh grade, Nell ran on the boys' track team, but by eighth grade, Nell wanted to run with the girls' team. Mark and Nina challenged her, but she stuck to her guns. She knew where she needed to be, albeit this was unchartered waters for her parents, many of her teammates and their families, as well as the community.

SURPRISES AND CHANGES

During this time, the family didn't think about Nell's transition every day, nor was it something that was top of mind. Nina explained, "We were busy with the schedule of parenting three kids, full-time jobs, and participating in after-school and work activities."

However, sometimes unexpected surprises popped up. Nina shared that during one of the early summers in this journey, Nell came into the kitchen to let her know where she was going. She was in a dress and had stuffed her bra. This caused Nina to chuckle, but she knew that if she was taken aback about the amount of tissue Nell had used, others would be, too. Nina anticipated many talks as a mother, but this one forced her to think quickly on her feet. She approached Nell for a quick chat. "Not all women, nor young girls your age, look that way," she told Nell. "You may want to tone it down a little bit." Nell agreed and removed some of the padding.

Nell continued to dress as she always had dressed to go to school—in athletic shorts and a sweatshirt—but varied her attire for special occasions and when around the right group of friends. She grew her hair out and left it natural, which is wavy like her mother's hair and strawberry blonde.

Going into high school, Nell wanted to continue to play on the girls' teams, which meant she would be the first transgender student to play on a varsity sport at that school. Because the current state laws allow trans students to play sports that support their gender identity, this wasn't considered an issue. Due to this and a supportive coach, Nell's participation was challenged directly only once: During a period of three years, one team refused to play because of a transgender player.

With Nell's unwavering decisiveness and sense of self over several years, she and her parents decided to explore options for the next step, which is to medically transition into a female. This was allowed in their state if supported by the parents or guardian. Mark and Nina said, "Everything happened very quickly. It was like we were in the right place at the right time in history." By the fall of 2022, Nell started using estrogen patches and a testosterone blocker.

NELL'S PROGRESS

Fast forward to today, and Nell's confidence is undeniable. Her academics are slating her for the top of her class, with aspirations to study genetic engineering. In addition, her performance on the soccer field has earned respect. Nell's experience has reshaped her entire family.

Always supporters, yet protective, Nina and Mark have learned to navigate their fears as parents. "We worried so much about protecting her that we sometimes got it wrong," said Mark. Her siblings, Wren and Oliver, have embraced her transformation from the beginning. Nina explained, "Wren was like *whatever,* and Oliver had trans friends in school, so they were okay with it. This experience has taught us how to live authentically. Our family's dynamic has grown stronger through this."

Throughout the Fredericks' story, the *Look Up* connection consisted of their two-fold positive advantages: 1) Nell's inspiring self-confidence and 2) the ideal time and place for her situation.

1) How many of us can say that at eleven, thirteen, or twenty-one we were as self-assured as Nell? She realized she was on the wrong life path and opted for a detour, regardless of the roadblocks it would cause. Nell took her obstacle and made it a springboard to her complete self.

2) Nell and her family's challenges were, and still are, far more well received because of where they live in the U.S. Certain locales have a cultural Zeitgeist for transgender kids, young adults, and even adults. That said, many places have a long way to go to accept a transgender person as easily as someone who is left-handed or an individual with red hair.

Although Nell is eager to start college, she plans to make surgery the next step in her transition. After high school graduation she will have it done, then take a gap year to fully heal.

Nell's story is not about being trans; it's about being true to herself. "She just wants to be seen as who she is," Nina said. "That's what we all want—to be accepted for who we truly are."

ABOUT THE FREDERICKS

The Fredericks are a happy family of five humans and three fur babies. Both Mark and Nina work full time within a rural area in Northen California. Oliver is studying theater at a public university in Oregon. Nell is about to graduate high school and gearing up for her gap year. Wren is still in high school and playing soccer. To spread more awareness about the transgender movement, the family suggested these resources: Camp Wild Heart Podcast and *American Teenager: How Trans Kids Are Surviving Hate and Finding Joy in a Turbulent Era* by Nico Lang.

EPILOGUE:
A GLOBAL TAPESTRY OF RESILIENCE

All of these stories, from Vietnam to Wisconsin, from Hawaii to Cuba and beyond, no matter the place, culture, or circumstance, show that human resilience is a shared experience. Each story contributes to a larger picture of *Look Up*, highlighting the power of perspective and how the human spirit can help us survive and grow. A common thread is that we don't control this thing called life; it's going to throw us all curveballs. How we harness our true power is paramount.

It's easy to fall into old habits, complain about roadblocks, and throw adult temper tantrums. However, we can take the most important step toward our growth by embracing the two components of the *Look Up* mantra: 1) Be in the moment and 2) Find the upside in any obstacle.

Following are a few conclusions from our contributors' stories:

"Looking up to me means taking on a new perspective; looking up and around, *not* down."
– Rhonda McGowan

"Even in the face of unimaginable loss, we can look up, find light, and move forward....When you lose everything, you realize what truly matters. It's not the things; it's the people, the connections, the memories."
– Pamela Reader

"War puts you into this very moment for survival. If you don't find an upside and *Look Up,* you develop PTSD.
I was able to look up and experience post-traumatic transformation, when I could have expected the reverse."
– Helena Summer

Just like all these real-life sheroes, heroes, and badasses, you, too, can overcome and thrive against the odds. May this global tapestry or mosaic of resilience inspire you in your journey, no matter the level of your challenges.

Here's to looking up!

ACKNOWLEDGMENTS

Thanks to my clan and famigos!
I couldn't have done this without you!

Mom, Dad, and my PIC
Adriana, Elaine, Caris, Diana, Karol, Will, Bryan
Norman, Patsy, Chrissie, Vila, Kris, Rose, Aerial

A standing ovation for the contributors to this book:

Pamela Reader and Family (Maui)
Sage Adderley (Washington State, Hawaii,)
Mary McQuain (Connecticut, Arizona)
The McCombs (South Florida, Oklahoma)
Amy Becker (Wisconsin)
Chong Hang (Laos, Thailand, Wisconsin, California, Carolinas)
Helena Summer (Yugoslavia, Croatia, London, Hawaii, Texas)
Cristina and Emily Rodriguez (Cuba, Michigan, Florida)
Catherine Francis (Massachusetts)
Lorna, Lesley, and Linda (Minnesota, Indiana, Pennsylvania)
Dr. Derek Riebau (Wisconsin, Tennessee)
Michelle Mann (Arizona)
P.J. (Arizona, Japan, Las Vegas)

Mariah Forster Olson (Wisconsin)

Rhonda McGowan (Wisconsin)

Heidi Love (Maine, Philly, Galapagos Islands, French Polynesia)

Ridhish Dadbhawla (India, New York, California)

Dr. Brooke Foreman (Texas, Hawaii)

Tom Thibodeau (Wisconsin)

Krystle Knight (Tennessee)

Andrew Krichels (Massachusetts, New York, Tennessee)

The Fredericks (Northern California)

Cheers to the A Team:

Peggy Henrikson, Heart and Soul Editing

Yvonne Parks of *PearCreative.ca*

Zach Levendorf of *LevyMediaMarketing.com*

Flavia Santos of *Designarie.com*

CONNECT WITH HEIDI

You're invited to connect with Heidi on her website *https:// heidisiefkas.com*, Facebook, LinkedIn, YouTube, X, and Instagram. You can find her other books on Amazon in print, eBook, and audio versions:

When All Balls Drop: The Upside of Losing Everything
With New Eyes: The Power of Perspective
Cubicle to Cuba: Desk Job to Dream Job

WHAT PEOPLE SAY ABOUT
HEIDI'S BOOKS

When All Balls Drop:
The Upside of Losing Everything

"A powerful chronicle of ultimate change and recovery."
– D. Donovan, *Midwest Book Review*

"A compelling story of tenacity, humor and accomplishment."
– Jordan Rich, WBZ CBS Boston

With New Eyes: The Power of Perspective

"Feisty and thought-provoking."
– *Midwest Book Review*

"You'll come away looking at the small details in your own life with a little more clarity. For a memoir, there may be no higher praise."
– *Self-Publishing Review*

Cubical to Cuba: Desk Job to Dream Job

"A spirited and page-turning read."
– *Self-Publishing Review*

"Inspiring, uplifting; will make you smile
throughout your time reading this book!"
– **Cynthia A. Stephenson**

WHAT PEOPLE SAY ABOUT
HEIDI'S TALKS

"Insightful and inspiring—Your audience will be completely engaged and follow along effortlessly on her journey through life's adventures. You will feel sad, encouraged, and happy, leaving with tools to help you through your challenges."

– Ellen Latham, M.S.
Founder of Orange Theory Fitness Franchise

"A dynamic speaker with a unique ability to take a traumatic life event and create a positive light. Her interactive approach allows her audience to connect with her message."

– Yvonne Hasse
VP of Suits, Stilettos and Lipstick

To schedule a presentation and/or event with Heidi, please contact her through: *heidi@hidenseekmedia.com.*

ABOUT THE AUTHOR

Heidi Siefkas is an author, speaker, and adventurer. Originally from small-town Wisconsin, Heidi hangs her hat in Nashville, Tennessee. However, as an adventurer, Heidi is always in search of her next challenge and story. She has authored four books: *When All Balls Drop, With New Eyes, Cubicle to Cuba,* and *Look Up,* which illustrates the power of her mantra. You're invited to check out her TEDx Talks on YouTube: "Overcoming Obstacles and Evolving to Life 2.0" and "The Life Hack the Gurus Don't Tell You About."

Connect with Heidi at *www.heidisiefkas.com*
and on LinkedIn, Facebook, Instagram, and X.